John Richardson Illingworth

Personality, Human and Divine

John Richardson Illingworth

Personality, Human and Divine

ISBN/EAN: 9783337366636

Printed in Europe, USA, Canada, Australia, Japan

Cover: Foto ©Paul-Georg Meister /pixelio.de

More available books at **www.hansebooks.com**

PERSONALITY

HUMAN AND DIVINE

BEING

THE BAMPTON LECTURES

FOR THE YEAR 1894

BY

J. R. ILLINGWORTH, M.A.

Ἦν ἄρα ὡς ἔοικε πάντων μέγιστον μαθημάτων τὸ γνῶναι αὑτόν· ἑαυτὸν γάρ τις ἐὰν γνῴη Θεὸν εἴσεται.
Clem. Alex.

London
MACMILLAN AND CO, Ltd.
NEW YORK: THE MACMILLAN COMPANY
1898

First Edition, October 1894
Reprinted, December 1894, 1895, 1896, 1898

OXFORD: HORACE HART, PRINTER TO THE UNIVERSITY

EXTRACT

FROM THE LAST WILL AND TESTAMENT

OF THE LATE

REV. JOHN BAMPTON,

CANON OF SALISBURY.

―――" I give and bequeath my Lands and Estates
"to the Chancellor, Masters, and Scholars of the
"University of Oxford for ever, to have and to
"hold all and singular the said Lands or Estates
"upon trust, and to the intents and purposes
"hereinafter mentioned; that is to say, I will and
"appoint that the Vice-Chancellor of the University
"of Oxford for the time being shall take and
"receive all the rents, issues, and profits thereof,
"and (after all taxes, reparations, and necessary
"deductions made) that he pay all the remainder
"to the endowment of eight Divinity Lecture
"Sermons, to be established for ever in the said
"University, and to be performed in the manner
"following:

"I direct and appoint, that, upon the first Tuesday
"in Easter Term, a Lecturer may be yearly chosen
"by the Heads of Colleges only, and by no others,
"in the room adjoining to the Printing-House, be-
"tween the hours of ten in the morning and two in
"the afternoon, to preach eight Divinity Lecture
"Sermons, the year following, at St. Mary's in

"Oxford, between the commencement of the last month in Lent Term, and the end of the third week in Act Term.

"Also I direct and appoint, that the eight Divinity Lecture Sermons shall be preached upon either of the following Subjects—to confirm and establish the Christian Faith, and to confute all heretics and schismatics—upon the divine authority of the holy Scriptures—upon the authority of the writings of the primitive Fathers, as to the faith and practice of the primitive Church—upon the Divinity of our Lord and Saviour Jesus Christ—upon the Divinity of the Holy Ghost—upon the Articles of the Christian Faith, as comprehended in the Apostles' and Nicene Creed.

"Also I direct, that thirty copies of the eight Divinity Lecture Sermons shall be always printed, within two months after they are preached; and one copy shall be given to the Chancellor of the University, and one copy to the Head of every College, and one copy to the Mayor of the city of Oxford, and one copy to be put into the Bodleian Library; and the expense of printing them shall be paid out of the revenue of the Land or Estates given for establishing the Divinity Lecture Sermons; and the Preacher shall not be paid, nor be entitled to the revenue, before they are printed.

"Also I direct and appoint, that no person shall be qualified to preach the Divinity Lecture Sermons, unless he hath taken the degree of Master of Arts at least, in one of the two Universities of Oxford or Cambridge; and that the same person shall never preach the Divinity Lecture Sermons twice."

PREFACE

An apologetic preface is always apt to savour of unreality, as it naturally invites the criticism that what requires an apology need never have been printed. Yet it is difficult to publish anything upon a serious subject without some expression of one's sense of its inadequacy. I will merely say, therefore, that the following lectures make no claim to originality; they are simply an attempt to arrange and summarize what has already been expressed with greater amplitude and fuller authority elsewhere; in the hope of attracting some, whose leisure in these eager days may be limited, to reconsider the important question with which they deal. Their main contention is that, whereas physical science has nowise weakened, critical philosophy has distinctly strengthened the claim—the immemorial claim—of human personality, to be a spiritual thing; and, as such, the highest category under which we can conceive of God. And as this conception would lead us to expect a progressive revelation, the evidence of such a revelation is briefly traced, and its culmination in the Incarnation vindicated. Such notes have been appended as may serve to illustrate and emphasize the main position of the lectures, by reference to authorities where their various issues are more adequately discussed.

CONTENTS

LECTURE I.

DEVELOPMENT OF THE CONCEPTION OF HUMAN PERSONALITY.

	PAGE
1. The sense of personality a gradual growth	6
2. Its pre-Christian recognition imperfect	7
3. Its final definition due to Christianity	8
4. Epochs in its evolution marked by Augustine, Luther, Kant	14
5. Personality the gateway of all knowledge	25

LECTURE II.

ANALYSIS OF THE CONCEPTION OF HUMAN PERSONALITY.

1. Characteristics of personality, (1) reason, (2) will, (3) love	29
2. Its unity	30
3. Its identity	40
4. Its reality	43
5. Its spirituality	45
6. Its mystery	52

LECTURE III.

DEVELOPMENT OF THE CONCEPTION OF DIVINE PERSONALITY.

		PAGE
1.	The sense of Divine Personality (1) vague, but (2) universal	54
2.	It is progressively refined by	
	(1) Greek Philosophers . .	59
	(2) Hebrew Prophets	65
	(3) Christian Fathers	66
3.	It culminates in the doctrine of the Trinity .	67
4.	Belief in a personal God is therefore an instinctive judgement progressively justified by reason	76

LECTURE IV.

ANALYSIS OF THE CONCEPTION OF DIVINE PERSONALITY.

1.	Belief in a Personal God	
	(1) Primarily instinctive . . .	81
	(2) Secondarily rational . . .	82
2.	Thus the so-called 'proofs' are analyses of a fundamental instinct	83
3.	They are	
	(1) Cosmological, i.e. argument from a First Cause	84
	(2) Teleological, i.e. argument from design in nature . . .	93

  (3) Ontological, i.e. argument from the reality of thought . . . 100
  (4) Moral, i.e. argument from the sense of freedom, combined with that of obligation 103

LECTURE V.

MORAL AFFINITY NEEDFUL FOR THE KNOWLEDGE OF A PERSON.

1. Moral disposition necessary
  (1) For pursuit of science . . . 114
  (2) For knowledge of a friend . . 116
2. Knowledge of God must follow the same analogy, involving
  (1) Sincerity 120
  (2) Purification 121
  (3) Penitence 122
3. Conversely, God's self-revelation must be conditioned by man's moral and spiritual capacity. 124
4. This analogy confirmed by the 'personal experience' of holy men in every age . 132

LECTURE VI.

RELIGION IN THE PREHISTORIC PERIOD.

1. Personality implies desire of self-communication 138
2. Hence a revelation is antecedently probable . 139

	PAGE
3. Analogy points to its being gradual	140
4. The 'antiquity of man' no obstacle to this belief	143
5. The strength of 'customary' religion a confirmation of it	148
6. Myth a possible vehicle of primitive revelation	154
7. Polemical and philosophical views of pagan religion contrasted	161

LECTURE VII.

RELIGION IN PRE-CHRISTIAN HISTORY.

1. The ethnic religions possess 'notes' of revelation, e.g.	168
(1) Their hold upon mankind	169
(2) Their religious books	170
(3) Their belief in inspiration	171
2. The Hebrew religion claims a pre-eminent degree of inspiration, and justifies its claim	173
(1) By its contemporary character	174
(2) By its teleological character in relation to Christianity	175
(3) By the present influence of its Scriptures	181
3. Historical criticism cannot affect inspiration as a fact of experience	183

LECTURE VIII.

JESUS CHRIST THE DIVINE AND HUMAN PERSON.

	PAGE
1. The Incarnation the crowning proof of Divine Personality	192
2. The reasons for Its rejection really *a priori* .	192
3. These rest upon a materialistic conception of human personality which is untenable .	193
4. The *a posteriori* evidences in Its favour invincibly strong	196
5. It involves the doctrine of the Trinity in which our incomplete personality recognizes its archetype.	212

NOTES.

LECTURE I.

Note 1. Things new and old	217
2. Science and Theology equally anthropomorphic	219

LECTURE II.

Note 3. The introspective method . . .	222
4. Self-consciousness	224
5. Desire	226
6. Self-determination or freewill. . .	227

		PAGE
NOTE 7.	Unity of the Ego or self	233
8.	Personality the ultimate reality	236
9.	Matter an abstraction, and Materialism therefore impossible	238
10.	Personality a mystery	240

LECTURE III.

NOTE 11.	Positive and Negative Theology	242
12.	Personality predicable of God	243
13.	Inadequate conceptions necessarily illusory	246

LECTURE IV.

NOTE 14.	Theistic arguments	249
15.	The argument from the 'consensus gentium'	249
16.	The cosmological argument	251
17.	The teleological argument	255
18.	The ontological argument	257
19.	The moral argument	260

LECTURE V.

NOTE 20.	Morality the condition of spiritual insight	264

LECTURE VI.

NOTE 21.	Primitive man	265
22.	Natural religion	266

Lecture VII.

Note 23. Ethnic inspiration 267

Lecture VIII.

Note 24. The Incarnation 268
      25. The supernatural dignity of humanity . 270
      26. The conceptions of Divine and human personality vary together . . . 271
      27. Psychological illustrations of the doctrine of the Trinity 272

PERSONALITY HUMAN AND DIVINE

LECTURE I

DEVELOPMENT OF THE CONCEPTION OF HUMAN PERSONALITY

WHEN Xenophanes, in a passage now almost too familiar for quotation, first brought the charge of what is called anthropomorphism against religion, he initiated a mode of criticism which has not yet grown old. Again and again in subsequent history the same charge has been made and met; yet it survives, and in the present day is being continually urged, as a plea for the adoption of agnostic opinions. 'The lions, if they could have pictured a god,' says the old Greek thinker, 'would have pictured him in fashion like a lion; the horses like a horse; the oxen like an ox'; and man, it is implied, with no more justification, as inevitably considers him a magnified man. In our own day Matthew Arnold has employed his graceful pen to the same effect, though with less than his usual grace; and still more recent critics have reiterated the complaint. Meanwhile, as the phenomena of savage belief, with which we are now so well acquainted, may be easily adduced in favour of a similar conclusion, the reflections of *Caliban upon Setebos* have come to be regarded in many minds as at once an adequate illustration and complete condemnation of all theology.

Now the plausibility, and therefore the malignity, of this fallacy consists in the fact that it is half a truth; and as there can be no question of its immense prevalence in contemporary thought, nor of its disintegrating effect upon religion, and through religion upon society, an apology will hardly be needed for one more attempt to reconsider the argument from human to divine personality. This can, of course, only be done in outline, if it is to be done within moderate compass: but outlines—mere outlines—are not infrequently of use, as enabling us to estimate in a single survey the number, the variety, the proportion, the reciprocal interdependence of the diverse elements in a cumulative proof. They supply that synoptic view which, while immersed in the controversial pursuit of details, we are apt to lose, and which is nevertheless essential to our judging the details aright, as parts of one articulate whole.

Accordingly, the object of the following pages is to review our reasons for believing in a Personal

God; reasons in which, from the nature of the case, there is no novelty, and which have been stated and restated time out of mind; but which each generation, as it passes, needs to see exhibited afresh, in their relation to its own peculiar modes of thought[1]. This will involve a brief analysis of what we mean by personality; and as the present fulness of that meaning has only been acquired by slow degrees, we shall need first to cast a glance over the principal stages of its development.

Man lives first, and thinks afterwards. Not only as an infant does he breathe and take nourishment and grow, long before the dawn of conscious reason; but his reason, even when developed, can only act upon experience, that is upon something which has already been lived through. He makes history by his actions, before he can reflect upon it and write it. He takes notice of the facts of nature before he can compare and criticize and shape them into science; while history and science in their turn supply material for further thinking, and are examined and sifted and generalized and gathered up into philosophy. And though, of course, reason has an eye to the future, and works with the view of preparing for fresh developments of life, its foresight must spring from insight; it can only predict what is to come by discovering the law of the phenomena, the formula of the

[1] See note I.

curve, the lie of the strata in the past. It follows from this that thought is always in arrear of life; for life is in perpetual progress, and, while we are reflecting on what happened yesterday, some further thing is happening to-day. 'When philosophy,' says Hegel, with a touch of sadness—'when philosophy paints its grey in grey, some one shape of life has meanwhile grown old: and grey in grey, though it brings it into knowledge, cannot make it young again. The owl of Minerva does not start upon its flight until the evening twilight has begun to fall.' Consequently no system of philosophy, no intellectual explanation of things, can ever become adequate or final. Reason is incessantly at work, to render more and more explicit the implicit principles, or principles which are implied in life; but there is always an unexplained residuum, an unfathomed abyss in the background, from which new and unforeseen developments may at any moment, and do from time to time, arise.

On the other hand, it must not rashly be concluded from this, that thought is an impotent abstraction, a pale imitation of the full-blooded reality of life, like a faded flower, or sad memory of pleasure past and gone. We do indeed in the course of our thinking often deal with abstractions, isolated aspects of things—such as quantity, quality, and the like; but only as a means to an end, a subordinate phase in an organic process. Thought as a whole does not tend towards the abstract, but towards the concrete. It issues, as we have seen, from the lesser to reissue in larger forms of life, as fruit issues from a flower to reissue in fresh seed of flowers. It penetrates the dull mass of life till the whole becomes luminous and glows. It is an inseparable element of the highest life; or rather it is life raised to its highest power. Thus a man lives, and as he lives reflects upon his life; with the result that he comes by degrees to understand what is within him; his capacities, his powers, the meaning of his actions; and as he does so he ceases to be the creature of mere outward circumstance, or mere inward instinct: he knows what he is about, and can direct and concentrate his energies; his life becomes fuller, richer, more real, more concrete, because more conscious; his thought is not a mirror which passively reflects his life, but, on the contrary, his life is the image, the picture, the music, the more or less adequate language of his thoughts. Or again, a great historical movement, in religion or in politics, will often begin blindly; stuttering, stammering, striking at random; till in process of time it gradually awakes to its own true meaning, and grows intelligent, articulate, effective, the recognized expression of a grand idea. Thus in a sense we may say truly that thought realizes or invests things with more complete reality, and so that only what is rational is real.

Now in nothing, perhaps, is this order of development from life to thought, from fact to explanation, better exhibited, than in the process by which man has come to recognize what we call his personality, all that is potentially or actually contained within himself—in a word what it means to be a man. Uneducated races, as we know, tend to personify or animate external nature; and though this, of course, implies some consciousness of their own personality, it is obviously an incomplete and unreflective consciousness; for it has not yet reached that essential stage in definition which consists in separating a thing from what it is not. This distinction of the personal from the impersonal region, or, in other language, of persons from things, would appear to have been a gradual process. And even when we reach the climax of ancient civilization, in Greece and Rome, there is no adequate sense, either in theory or practice, of human personality as such. This may be seen, without at present pausing to define the term, by looking at two of its obvious characteristics. Personality, as we understand it, is universal in its extension or scope—that is, it must pertain to every human being as such, making him man; and it is one in its intention or meaning—that is, it is the unifying principle, or, to use a more guarded expression, the name of the unity in which all a man's attributes and functions meet, making him an individual self. And on both these points the theory and practice of the ancient world was deficient. Aristotle, its best exponent, views some men as born to be savages (φύσει βάρβαροι), and others as destined by nature to be slaves (φύσει δοῦλοι), whom he further regards as living machines (ἔμψυχα ὄργανα), and women, apparently in all seriousness, as nature's failures in the attempt to produce men. And Plato before him, despite of those flashes of insight which are beyond his own and most subsequent ages, had, on the whole, taught much to the same effect. And this is an accurate philosophical summary of the practice of pre-Christian society. On the other hand, in his psychology and ethics Aristotle fails to unify human nature. In the former he leaves an unsolved dualism between the soul and its organism, the active and receptive faculties (νοῦς ποιητικός and νοῦς παθητικός); while in the latter he has no clear conception of the will, and hardly any of the conscience—the two faculties or functions which alone identify our various scattered emotions and activities with our real self. And here too he is only reflecting the facts of contemporary society, which was characterized by a fatal divorce between the various departments of life, the public and the private, the moral and the religious, the intellectual and the sensual; excellence in one region being easily allowed to compensate for licence or failure in another. Here and there may be found sporadic exceptions to this as to all other historic generalizations; but they are few and far between, and nowhere rarer than in the class where we should most naturally have expected to meet them—the professed teachers of philosophy. As a rule it is beyond dispute that neither the universality nor the unity of human personality, its two most obviously essential features, were adequately understood in pre-Christian ages; though stoicism was beginning to pave the way for their recognition. But the advent of Christianity created a new epoch both in the development and recognition of human personality. Its Founder lived a life and exercised a personal attraction, but is expressly reported to have told His followers that the full meaning of that life and its attraction would not be understood till He was gone: 'When He, the Spirit of Truth, is come, ... He shall glorify me, for He shall take of mine and shall show it unto you.' 'He shall teach you all things, and bring to your remembrance all that I said unto you.' The fact of the unique life came first, the new personality; and then the gradual explanation of the fact, in the doctrine of the person of Christ; an order which is already observable in the contrast that we see between the synoptic and the fourth gospels. In the same way the early Christians began by feeling a new life within them, due, as they believed, to their being in spiritual contact with the living person of their Lord; and enabling them to say 'I live, yet not I, Christ liveth in me.' 'Let us therefore do all things as becomes those who have God dwelling in them [1].' Then they went on, according to their capacity and the necessities of the time, to give a reason for the hope that was in them. And even in so doing we notice that the first apologists chiefly appeal to the striking contrast between the life which Christians led and that of the cruel, immoral, superstitious, sad, suicidal world around them. Only as time went on, and Christianity came to assume a place of prominence in the great intellectual centres of the world—Antioch, Athens, Ephesus, Alexandria and Rome—were the intellectual presuppositions of this life unfolded; and the Christian theology—that is, the authorized explanation of the Christian facts which had begun with the writings of St. Paul and of St. John—was thus by slow degrees developed.

Our present object, it must be remembered, is purely historical, and we need not therefore pause either to defend or criticize the precise form which the development of Christian doctrine assumed. Some development or other must have taken place; for the world cannot stand still. Thoughtful men must meditate upon the things

[1] Ignat. *Ep. ad Ephes.* 15.

which they believe, and endeavour to give articulate expression to what is implicitly contained in the principles by which they live; while the missionary desire to commend their creed to other minds, and the consequent encounter with intellectual opposition, will naturally increase the need of theological definition. Questions must be asked and answers given; and sooner or later a great religious movement must be philosophically explained. But the philosophical explanation of Christianity, despite of all that has been crudely urged against its metaphysical subtlety, was eminently conservative, sober-minded, slow. The air was full of wild and seductive systems of speculation; and individual Christians were diverging into strange opinions upon all sides. And when the general councils were called together, to correct them, there was indeed much to be deplored in the historical circumstances of their assembling, as well as the tone and temper of many of their members. Yet all this does but emphasize the comparative moderation of their collective voice. Their undoubted purpose, as viewed by themselves, was to define and guard, and to define only in order to guard, what they conceived to be the essence of Christianity, the divine humanity of Jesus Christ, and that with a strictly practical aim. For personal union with the living Christ was felt to be the secret of the Christian life. And had Christ been a mere man as with the Ebionites, or a mere appearance as with the Docetes, or a Gnostic emanation, or an Arian demigod, the reality of that union would have vanished. 'Our all is at stake,' Athanasius truly said, in justification of his lifelong conflict. This was the real contribution of the general councils to human history; the more and more explicit reassertion of the Incarnation, as a mystery indeed, but as a fact. The various heresies which attempted to make the Incarnation more intelligible, in reality explained it away; while council after council, though freely adopting new phraseology and new conceptions, never claimed to do more than give explicit expression to what the Church from the beginning had implicitly believed. And we may fairly maintain that modern research has made the historic accuracy of this claim even more apparent, than when Bull defended it against Petavius, or Waterland against Clarke. Thus, then, Christian theology arose, like all other human thought, in meditation upon a fact of experience—the life and teaching of Jesus Christ; and having arisen, reacted, also like other human thought, upon the fact which it explained, illuminating, intensifying, realizing the significance of that fact. Opinions, of course, differ upon the value of this result, according as men believe or deny that it was due to the guidance of the Spirit of God. But our present concern is with a point of history, which admits of no denial, an inevitable but indirect and incidental consequence of the theological ferment of the first Christian centuries, viz. the introduction into the world of a deeper if not an altogether new conception of human personality. God had become man, according to the Christian creed, and the theological interpretation and application of this fact threw a new light upon the whole of human nature. Men may deny its right to have done so, but they cannot deny the fact that it did so, which is all with which we are now concerned. Not only had human nature in an unique instance been personally united to God; but the whole human race, whether male or female, barbarian or Scythian, bond or free, were declared capable of a communicated participation in that union; and this at once threw a new light upon the depth of latent possibility, not only in the favoured few, but in man as such. Again, the holiness which this union demanded, and which was emphatically a new standard in the world, admitted of no dualism. Men were bidden to bring their entire nature into harmony with the law of conscience, focussing thereby their various and divergent faculties and thoughts and feelings in a central unity. The heterogeneous elements were forced into coherence. Man was unified. And further, the sense of responsibility and accountability, which all this implied, led to more elaborate examination of the will and its freedom (τὸ αὐτεξούσιον), while the clearer conviction of immortality and judgement emphasized the personal identity of man. Here, then, were the various factors of what we call personality, being gradually thought out. Nor was it only a work of thought. Man's personality was being actually developed. It was becoming deeper and more intense. A new type was appearing, and attempting to explain itself as it appeared. And meanwhile the Trinitarian controversies were ventilating the question of the relation of subject to object, the question upon which the nature of self-consciousness, and therefore of personality, depends. This took place mainly indeed in the ontological region, as was inevitable from the state of philosophy at the time, but still not without a sense that man was, metaphysically as well as otherwise, made in the image and likeness of God (εἰκὼν καὶ ὁμοίωσις). And though it was not till a later age that the results of this analysis were at all fully transferred from theology to psychology, yet the real foundations of our subsequent thought upon the point were undoubtedly laid in the first Christian centuries, and chiefly by Christian hands.

It is, of course, impossible to trace minutely the development of an idea whose elements gradually coalesced, as floating things are drawn together in the vortex of a stream. Many minds and many influences contributed to the result, while the monasteries provided homes for introspective meditation. But for convenience of summary and memory three names may perhaps be singled out, as at least typical, if not actually creative, of the chief epochs, through which the conception of personality has passed—Augustine, Luther, Kant.

Augustine had his predecessors, especially Origen and Tertullian, in their very different ways; but in introspective power he far surpasses them, as, for instance, when in the *Confessions* he sounds the abyss of his own being:

'I come to the spacious fields and palaces of memory, wherein are treasured unnumbered images of things of sense, and all our thoughts about them. . . . There in that vast court of memory are present to me heaven, earth, sea, and all that I can think upon, all that I have forgotten therein. There too I meet myself, and whatever I have felt and done, my experiences, my beliefs, my hopes and plans for the years to come. . . . Great is this power of memory, exceeding great, O God. Who has ever fathomed its abyss? And yet this power is mine, a part of my very nature, nor can I comprehend all that I myself really am. . . . Great is this power of memory, a wondrous thing, O my God, in all its depth and manifold immensity, and this thing is my mind, and this mind is myself. . . . Fear and amazement overcome me when I think of it. And yet men go abroad to gaze upon the mountains and the waves, the broad rivers, the wide ocean, the courses of the stars, and pass themselves, the crowning wonder, by[1].' If we compare such a passage with the famous Greek chorus in which the wonder of man's nature is described, wholly in terms of his external works, his stemming of the tides, his taming of the horse, his inventions, his contrivances, his arts, it may help us to realize the change which had passed over men's thoughts. But Augustine is no mere rhetorician; and elsewhere he speaks with more philosophical accuracy: 'Go not abroad, retire into thyself, for truth dwells in the inner man[2].' 'The mind knows best what is nearest to it, and nothing is nearer to the mind than itself[3].' 'We exist, and know that we exist, and love the existence and the knowledge; and on these three points no specious falsehood can deceive us... for without any misleading fallacies or fancies of the imagination, I am absolutely certain that I exist, and that I know and desire my own existence[4].' 'In knowing itself, the mind knows its own substantial existence (substantiam suam novit), and in its certainty of itself, it is certain of its own substantiality (de substantia sua)[5].'

Our present purpose is not critical but historical, and we need not, therefore, pause upon these statements except to point out the distinct development of self-analysis which they imply, and their natural

---

[1] Aug. *Confessions.*   [2] *De ver. rel.* 73.   [3] *De Trin.* 14. 7.
[4] *De Civ. Dei,* 11. 26.   [5] *De Trin.* 10. 16.

tendency to bear further fruit, in the congenial soil of those countless kindred minds which were to throng the cloister for the next thousand years, and issue at length in German mysticism and Luther.

The French mystics of the twelfth century and their followers, in reaction from the somewhat thin rationalism of their day, developed an emotional rather than an intellectual type of mysticism—which, with all its fervour and beauty, was not widely influential on the progress of thought. But with the German mystics, Eckhart, Tauler, Suso, the case was different. To begin with, the time was more fully ripe for their effective appearance. And further, they sprang from the great preaching order, and laboured, under the exigencies of the pulpit, to bring their meaning home to the mass of men; while the fact, that both preachers and hearers were of the subjective Teutonic race, gave that intellectual cast to their teaching which enabled it to influence all subsequent thought. We are only concerned here with their contribution to the development of personality; which consisted in emphasizing the intimacy and immediacy of the union between the soul and God. This was no more than had been taught in the earlier ages of Christianity, or than was justified in the philosophy of Albert the Great and St. Thomas Aquinas. But practically the tendency of the mediaeval church, with its over-use of sacerdotal and saintly mediation, had been to exaggerate the distance between God and man. Hence the significance of the mystical movement. But mysticism has always had its attendant danger—the danger of seeking union with God by obliteration of human limitations and human attributes on the one hand, and on the other of underestimating the human sense of guilt, that awful guardian of our personal identity. Hence, though it begins by deepening our sense of individuality, it often ends by drifting, both morally and intellectually, towards a Pantheism in which all individuality is lost. From this danger, with all their merits, the German mystics were not wholly free. And consequently Luther, who was profoundly influenced by them, without falling into their error, became the most effectual exponent of their central thought.

In saying this we are not concerned with his theology in general, but with the central thought which lay at the root of it all; a thought which he expressed in a more intelligible and, perhaps, on the whole a more guarded way than Eckhart, and for which he consequently secured a popularity such as Eckhart could never have attained. That thought was the natural affinity of the human soul, through all its sin, for God; and of God for the human soul; and the consequent possibility of an immediate relation between the two. He turned, as Dorner puts it, from the metaphysical to the moral attributes of God and man, culminating as they do in love; and proclaimed that here was the only ground for an intimate and in a measure intelligible union of the two. For it is the nature of a God whose essence is love to communicate Himself, and the nature of a man whose essence is the desire for love to be receptive of that communication (capax deitatis). The famous phrase 'justification by faith' is an attempt to express this thought. 'Faith,' he says in one place, 'is, if I may use the expression, creative of divinity; not, of course, in the substance of God, but in ourselves [1].' 'Faith has, strictly speaking, no object but Christ . . . . and it is this faith which lays hold of Christ and is clothed with Him (ornatur) which justifies [2].' 'Christ lives in me, He is my formal cause (is est mea forma) clothing my faith [3].' 'I am wont, in order to understand this better, to picture myself as having no quality in my heart that can be called faith or love, but in place of this I put Christ Himself, and say, "This is my righteousness."' This intimacy and immediacy of possible union between the soul and God was, of course, no theological novelty; but it had long vanished from the popular religion.

Luther re-emphasized it, with a vehemence to which the circumstances of the age contributed yet

---

[1] Luther, *in Gal.* ii. 16.   [2] Id. ii. 20.
[3] Id. *ad Brent. Ep.* (quoted by Newman, *Lect. on Justification*).

further emphasis; and, above all, he proclaimed it the basis of spiritual independence; the soul, which is the slave of God, being thereby free from all other slavery, to religious or philosophic authority, and external means of grace. The freedom of the human spirit through union with God became thus a familiar thought, a recognized principle, a controversial commonplace, in the mouths of many who had no inner experience of its truth. But, however paradoxically stated, abused, exaggerated, misapplied, its publication made an epoch in the world. It had previously been an esoteric doctrine. Luther proclaimed it from the housetop; and in so doing dignified and deepened the whole sense of personality in man.

So far, then, the development of the sense of personality was due to religious influence, monastic meditation continuing what the age of the great councils had begun. Man had viewed himself in the light of the Incarnation and all that the Incarnation implied; and as a consequence had come to have deeper conceptions of his own nature and its capacities; his unity, his indestructible identity, his inherent dignity, his wonderful possibilities and consequent worth. But the time came when the dogmatic basis upon which all this rested was cast into the crucible of criticism; for the question which in the middle ages had been seldom asked, and if asked suppressed, forced itself at last

to the front, with an importunate insistence—the question, 'Can man know God?' To meet this by reasoning, in any sort or form, from the personality of man to the personality of God, would be obviously impossible if the former conception itself had been chiefly derived from an illegitimate belief in the latter; and therefore a critical review of our faculties became necessary, which should discard all traditional authority, whether philosophic or religious, and examine human nature, by itself, to see what was really in it, what essential capabilities it possessed, and what were their inevitable and necessary limits. It was a fresh instance on a large scale of the universal order of development from life to thought, from fact to theory. The personality of man had been putting out new powers, and making for itself new claims, throughout the Christian ages; and now the time for afterthought had come, to see how far the result was justified.

This brings us to the critical philosophy of Kant. He too had his predecessors; notably, two in this particular inquiry, Descartes and Leibniz. Descartes, whether consciously or unconsciously, following out the thought of Augustine, had enunciated his famous maxim, 'Cogito ergo sum,' I think, therefore I am—Thought, that is to say, is the evidence of its own reality, and of the real existence of its thinker, the individual man. And

Leibniz, in his *Monadology*, had further emphasized the notion of individuality as involving both isolation from and relation to the whole outside universe; the isolation of separate, self-identical existence; the relation of sensitive and mental intercourse, as we should now say, though he himself used the very different and much less adequate term reflection, as in a mirror. But it was Kant who inaugurated the modern epoch in the treatment of personality. In the first place he analyzed self-consciousness, the power of separating oneself as a subject from oneself as an object, or, in other words, oneself as thinking from oneself as thought about; and showed how all knowledge is due to the activity of the subject, or ego, or self, in bringing the multiplicity of external facts or internal feelings into relation with its own central unity, and thereby into correlation with one another; with the important corollary that what the ego has no means of thus relating to itself cannot become an object of knowledge. And then in the moral region he went on to show how the ego, or self, has not only the power of making objects for its own understanding, but also the power of making objects for its own pursuit, motives for its own conduct; and is thus self-determining, or able to become a law to itself, and in this sense free. Further, despite of much subsequent controversy upon the point, it may be affirmed, without doubt, that he viewed these two aspects of personality as united by the inherent primacy of the practical over the speculative reason; denying to the latter the right of prosecuting its own exclusive interests, or trusting its own conclusions, in independence or contradiction of the interests and conclusions of the former. And, finally, he pointed out that all persons, in virtue of their inherent freedom, are ends in themselves, and never merely means to other ends. Their power of self-determination, of becoming a law to themselves, is inalienable; irresistibly compelling them to regard themselves as ends, ultimate objects of endeavour or development, and entitling them to such consideration from others. However much, therefore, they may minister to or sacrifice themselves for others, of their own free-will, they may never be degraded into passive instruments of another's power or pleasure, as if they were impersonal things. A person, then, for Kant, was a self-conscious and self-determining individual, and as such an end in himself—the source from which thought and conduct radiate, and the end whose realization thought and conduct seek. Subsequent thinkers have thrown further light upon personality. But they are at once too numerous and too various to be briefly reviewed. Moreover, while differing widely from each other, they have all agreed in accepting Kant as their necessary point of departure. They have developed him both critically and constructively; but they have not gone back behind him. It will be sufficient, therefore, for our present purpose to pause with Kant.

Our reason for dwelling upon this process, by which man has gradually arrived at the knowledge of his own personality, its range, its limits and its scope, is twofold. In the first place it is a needful prelude to the description of personality itself. Personality cannot be exhaustively analyzed, and cannot, therefore, be accurately defined. It can only be described from observation. And in describing anything which has a history, that history must be taken into account as constituting part of the full meaning of the thing. And in the second place the appeal to history is especially necessitated by the character of the inquiry which we have in hand, since the fact that human personality has been a thing of slow development, and its conscious recognition of itself slower still, must have an important bearing upon the inference from the nature of man to the nature of God. For, however instinctive and immediate that inference may at times have been, it is plain that the personality attributed to God can at no period have been more distinctly conceived than was its human analogue; and we shall not be surprised to find the former conception gradually modified as the latter has grown more clear. In a word, since man himself has been progressive, his notion of God must have been progressive also, and we must neither expect to find its later in its earlier, nor be content with its earlier in its later stages.

Man, then, is a person or a being of a particular constitution, which he has come to denote by the term personality. He has made some progress in self-analysis, yet is still far from understanding all that his own personality implies. But one thing is certain, that he cannot transcend his personality, he cannot get outside himself. All his knowledge is personal knowledge, and is qualified and coloured by the fact. 'Our being,' as Dr. Newman forcibly expresses it—'our being, with its faculties, mind and body, is a fact not admitting of question, all things being of necessity referred to it, not it to other things. If I may not assume that I exist, and in a particular way—that is, with a particular mental constitution—I have nothing to speculate about, and had better leave speculation alone. Such as I am, it is my all; this is my essential standpoint, and must be taken for granted; otherwise, thought is but an idle amusement not worth the trouble. There is no medium between using my faculties as I have them and flinging myself upon the external world, according to the random impulse of the moment, as spray upon the surface of the waves, and simply forgetting that I am. I am what I am, or I am nothing. . . . If I do not use myself I have no other self to use. My only business is to ascertain what I am, in order to put it to use. It is enough for the proof of the value and authority of any function which I possess to be able to pronounce that it is natural[1].'

Personality is thus the gateway through which all knowledge must inevitably pass. Matter, force, energy, ideas, time, space, law, freedom, cause, and the like, are absolutely meaningless phrases except in the light of our personal experience. They represent different departments of that experience, which may be isolated for the purposes of special study, as we separate a word from its context to trace its linguistic affinities, or pluck a flower from its root to examine the texture of its tissues. But when we come to discuss their ultimate relations to ourselves and to one another, or, in other words, to philosophize about them, we must remember that they are only known to us in the last resort, through the categories of our own personality, and can never be understood exhaustively till we know all that our personality implies. It follows that philosophy and science are, in the strict sense of the word, precisely as anthropomorphic as theology[2], since they are alike limited by the conditions of human personality, and controlled by the forms of thought which human personality provides.

[1] Newman, *Grammar of Assent*, ix. § 1.
[2] See note 2.

The fact that man is thus, in the phrase of Protagoras, the measure of all things, has been urged as a ground for scepticism from very ancient days; but such scepticism to be logical must also be universal, and apply equally to all regions of thought. Seeing, however, that science and common-sense are both agreed to reject this extreme conclusion, and to maintain that personal experience conveys true knowledge in their respective spheres, no antecedent objection can be raised against theology, on the ground that it rests on personal experience, and is therefore anthropomorphic. In all cases the experience in question must be critically tested; but in none is it invalidated by the mere fact that it is personal. For, in the words of an English Kantian of the older school, 'It is from the intense consciousness of our own real existence as persons that the conception of reality takes its rise in our minds: it is through that consciousness alone that we can raise ourselves to the faintest image of the supreme reality of God. What is reality, and what is appearance? is the riddle which philosophy has put forth, from the birthday of human thought; and the only approach to an answer has been a voice from the depths of the personal consciousness: "I think, therefore I am." In the antithesis between the thinker and the object of his thought—between myself and that which is related to me—we find the type and the source of the universal contrast between the one and the many, the permanent and the changeable, the real and the apparent. That which I see, that which I hear, that which I think, that which I feel, changes and passes away with each moment of my varied existence. I, who see and hear and think and feel, am the one continuous self, whose existence gives unity and connexion to the whole. Personality comprises all that we know of that which exists; relation to personality comprises all that we know of that which seems to exist. And when from the little world of man's consciousness and its objects we would lift up our eyes to the inexhaustible universe beyond, and ask to whom all this is related, the highest existence is still the highest personality; and the Source of all being reveals Himself by His name "I Am[1]."'

[1] Mansel, *Bampton Lectures*, Lect. iii.

LECTURE II

ANALYSIS OF THE CONCEPTION OF HUMAN PERSONALITY

WE cannot, strictly speaking, define personality, for the simple reason that we cannot place ourselves outside it. 'The " mystery " that belongs to it,' as Professor Green says, ' arises from its being the only thing, or a form of the only thing, that is real (so to speak) in its own right; the only thing of which the reality is not relative and derived. .... We can only know it by a reflection on it which is its own action; by analysis of the expression it has given to itself, in language, literature, and the institutions of human life; and by consideration of what that must be which has thus expressed itself.' Looked at analytically[1], then, the fundamental characteristic of personality is self-consciousness[2], the quality in a subject of becoming an object to itself, or, in Locke's language, 'considering itself as itself,' and saying 'I am I.' But as in the very act of becoming thus self-con-

---

[1] See note 3.   [2] See note 4.

scious I discover in myself desires [1], and a will [2], the quality of self-consciousness immediately involves that of self-determination, the power of making my desires an object of my will, and saying 'I will do what I desire.' But we must not fall into the common error of regarding thought, desire, and will, as really separable in fact, because we are obliged for the sake of distinctness to give them separate names. They are three faculties or functions of one individual, and, though logically separable, interpenetrate each other, and are always more or less united in operation. I cannot, for instance, pursue a train of thought, however abstract, without attention, which is an act of *will*, and involves a *desire* to attend. I cannot desire, as distinct from merely feeling appetite, like an animal, without *thinking* of what I desire, and *willing* to attain or to abstain from it. I cannot will without *thinking* of an object or purpose, and *desiring* its realization. There is, therefore, a synthetic unity in my personality or self; that is to say, not a merely numerical oneness, but a power of uniting opposite and alien attributes and characteristics with an intimacy which defies analysis. This unity is further emphasized by my sense of personal identity, which irresistibly compels me to regard myself as one and the same being, through all changes of time and circumstance, and thus

[1] See note 5.   [2] See note 6.

unites my thoughts and feelings of to-day with those of all my bygone years. I am thus one, in the sense of an active unifying principle, which can not only combine a multitude of present experiences in itself, but can also combine its present with its past. At the same time, with all my inclusiveness, I have also an exclusive aspect. 'Each self,' it has been well said, 'is a unique existence, which is perfectly impervious to other selves—impervious in a fashion of which the impenetrability of matter is a faint analogue[1].' Thus a person has at once an individual and an universal side. He is an unit that excludes all else, and yet a totality or whole with infinite powers of inclusion.

It is necessary to emphasize this unity of our personality, on account of its controversial importance. Of course in ordinary life we all take it for granted; but this very fact only makes people the more liable to be disturbed, when assured that it can be decomposed and explained away by modern physiological psychology. We cannot, therefore, lay too much stress upon the fact of its recognition by the general voice of both ancient and modern philosophy, as distinct from that of a small minority of scientific specialists, who have not really made any advance upon the position of Hume, or disposed of Kant's answer to Hume. It is a point, moreover, on which critical philosophy is at one

[1] Seth, *Hegelianism and Personality*, p. 216.

with common-sense, while its opponents who attempt to resolve the unity into a multiplicity of impressions and desires, which, but for that unity, would have nothing to be impressed upon or desired by, maintain a paradox quite as incredible to the multitude as to the philosopher. And, whatever we may think of the 'argument from universal consent' taken by itself, it must distinctly be allowed weight when it corroborates and is corroborated by philosophic analysis. 'We meet,' says Lotze, 'with the word "soul" in the languages of all civilized peoples; and this proves that the imagination of man must have had reasons of weight for its supposition, that there is an existence of some special nature underlying the phenomena of the inner life as their subject or cause.' Philosophers have differed in the phrases by which they have described this unity, as well as in their views of the precise way in which we are aware of it. But these differences do not alter their agreement upon the fact. Kant, indeed, though the foremost to assert the unity of self-consciousness, goes so far as to deny that we can legitimately infer from it the existence of the soul as a separate substance; but this denial, besides being qualified by what he says elsewhere, in his critique of the practical reason, turns upon his peculiar doctrine of noumena, or things in themselves, the least satisfactory part

---

[1] Lotze, *Metaphys.* § 238.

of his system. And, as Lotze remarks, 'The identity of the subject of inward experience is all that we require. So far as, and so long as, the soul knows itself as this identical subject, it is, and is named, simply for that reason, substance.... That which is not only conceived by others as unity in multiplicity, but knows and makes itself good as such, is, simply on that account, the truest and most indivisible unity there can be [1].' But, though we can afford to be indifferent as to whether the word substance shall be used in this connexion or not, we must be on our guard against the fallacy which supposes that our notion of substance is first derived from the external world, and can thence have been imported into ourselves. For this is preposterous in the strict sense of the term. It puts the cart before the horse. There can be no question whatever that our whole idea of substance, as the permanent substratum which underlies and connects a variety of attributes into that unity which we call a 'thing,' is derived exclusively from our own experience of a permanent self, underlying (or under*standing*) all our affections and manifestations. Whether, therefore, we describe this *understanding* self as a substance or not, it is the only source from whence the conception of substance can have been derived, and of whatever meaning it may possess.

[1] Lotze, *Metaphys.* § 244.

Again, our self-consciousness involves freedom, or the power of self-determination. Enough and to spare has been written on the freedom of the will, and it will be sufficient for our present purpose simply to summarize the situation. The freedom of the will, then, does not mean the ability to act without a motive, as some of its opponents still stupidly seem to suppose. But it does mean the ability to create or co-operate in creating our own motives, or to choose our motive, or to transform a weaker motive into a stronger by adding weights to the scale of our own accord, and thus to determine our conduct by our reason; whence it is now usually called the power of self-determination—a phrase to which St. Thomas very nearly approaches when he says, 'Man is determined by a combination of reason and appetite (appetitu rationali), that is, by a desire whose object is consciously apprehended by the reason as an end to be attained, and he is therefore self-moved.' For instance, I am hungry, and that is simply an animal appetite; but I am immediately aware of an ability to choose between gratifying my hunger with an unwholesome food because it is pleasant, or with an unpleasant food because it is wholesome, or abstaining from its gratification altogether for self-discipline or because the food before me is not my own. That is to say, I can present to my mind, on the occasion of appetite, pleasure, utility, goodness, as objects to be attained, and I can choose between them; nor is it to the point to say that I am determined by my character, for my character is only the momentum which I have gained by a number of past acts of choice, that is by my own past use of my freedom; and even so I am conscious that at the moment I *can* counteract my character, though morally certain that I have no intention so to do.

This is briefly what we mean by free-will; and it is a fact of immediate and universal consciousness, that is, of my own consciousness, corroborated by the like experience of all other men. When Bain compares it to a belief in witches (and the comparison is typical of many more), as being a fact of consciousness as long as it is believed, his misapprehension of the point at issue is almost ludicrous. For the sense of freedom is an immediate part of my consciousness. I cannot be conscious without it. I cannot tear it out. It lies at the very root of myself, and claims, with self-evidence, to be something *sui generis*, something unique. So obvious is this, that most even of those who regard it as a delusion are obliged to admit that it is a delusion from which there is no escape. Further, upon this sense of freedom all law and all morality depend. To deny this is to play with words. And law and morality abundantly verify the legitimacy of their basis by the progressive development in which they result. For you cannot gather figs of thistles, or a rational order of society from an irrational disease of mind. And, finally, the sense of freedom has maintained itself, from the dawn of history, against a spirit far more powerful than any which philosophy can raise—the spirit of remorse. What would not humanity, age after age, have given to be free from remorse? Yet remorse still stares us in the face, overshadowing our hearts with sadness and driving its countless victims into madness, suicide, despair, and awful forebodings of the after-world. Men would have exorcised it if they could; but they cannot. And remorse is only a darker name for man's conviction of his own free-will.

We ground our belief in freedom, then, on two things—its immediate self-evidence in consciousness and its progressive self-justification in morality—the way in which its moral results approve themselves to the universal reason of mankind; and we are confident that no contrary argument can be constructed without surreptitiously assuming what it attempts to disprove. Lucretius was obliged to allow his atoms the power of swerving. And when Hobbes defines the will as 'the last appetite in deliberation,' he concedes by the latter word what he intends to deny by the former. And so with the later necessitarians. Their analysis is more elaborate and possesses the attraction for certain minds of any attempt to explain the primary aspect of a thing ingeniously away. But they have been convicted again and again, either of ignoring the point at issue, or begging, in one phrase or other, the question to be proved; while their success, if it were possible, would only land them in the old dilemma, that by invalidating consciousness they invalidate all power of reasoning, and with it the value of their own conclusions. 'Non ragioniam di lor.'

But will acts, as we have seen, upon the material supplied by desire; and this desire is a coessential element in our personality. Desire is the form which appetite necessarily takes in a rational being; it is appetite consciously directed to an end which reason presents, and may be called self-conscious appetite (the 'appetitus rationalis' of St. Thomas). And desire is, broadly speaking, of two kinds, desire of acquisition and desire of action, or, in other words, of food and exercise. We desire to incorporate and to assimilate with ourselves the various contents of our material, moral, and intellectual environment—as our food, our furniture, our property, our means of pleasure and of virtue and of knowledge. And we also desire to project ourselves into and modify that environment, by exercising our wealth or power or skill or influence or mind upon it. And, though these two processes of reception and action are often regarded as independent functions, it is important to notice that in fact they interpenetrate each other. An activity of the organism is involved in the simplest sensation, and more obviously in our every emotional and intellectual acquisition; no experience being purely passive. And, on the other hand, every action must be stimulated by a motive; and though reason, as we have seen, plays an important part in the constitution of this motive, the receptive faculties contribute the material of which the motive is to be made. Now this twofold process of desire, acquisitive and active, irresistibly impels us into communion with other persons. We are so constituted that we cannot regard inanimate property, uncommunicated knowledge, unreciprocated emotion, solitary action otherwise than as means to an end. We press on through it all, till we have found persons like ourselves with whom to share it, and then we are at rest. Thus all persons are ends to us, when compared with impersonal things, but in different degrees. For we have various desires, and each of them conducts us into a different kind of connexion with other persons. We may be more passive and receive sympathy from them, or more active and exercise influence over them. We may desire to share with them our pleasures, or our perplexities, or our work, or to exchange with them social amenities or intellectual ideas. And in all these ways they may represent ends to us, but still, in a sense, only partial ends; satisfying, that is, some one class of our desires, some one mode of our activity, some one department of our complex being. But we instinctively seek more than this. We require to find in other persons an end in which our entire personality may rest. And this is the relationship of love. Its intensity may admit of degrees, but it is distinguished from all other affections or desires, by being the outcome of our whole personality. It is our very self, and not a department of us, that loves. And what we love in others is the personality or self, which makes them what they are. We love them for their own sake. And love may be described as the mutual desire of persons for each other as such; the mode in which the life of desire finds its climax, its adequate and final satisfaction.

These, then, are the constituent elements of personality, as such—self-consciousness, the power of self-determination, and desires which irresistibly impel us into communion with other persons—or, in other words, reason, will, and love. These are three perfectly distinct and distinguishable functions, but they are united, as we have seen, by being the functions of one and the selfsame subject[1], and gain a peculiar character from this very fact. They are the thoughts of a being that

[1] See note 7.

wills and loves, the will of a being that loves and thinks, the love of a being that thinks and wills; and each attribute may be said to express the whole being, therefore, in terms of that attribute.

But in speaking thus of personality as a thing that can be analyzed, as if it were inanimate or abstract, we must not forget that in fact it is essentially alive, and can only be known as living; so that it is, perhaps, better described as an energy than as a substance. It lives and grows and develops character, as the will selects and appropriates to itself, or exerts its influence upon, the various material supplied by reason and desire. Consequently, there can be no stage in its existence when personality does not imply character, for which, indeed, in popular language it has almost become a synonym—as when we speak of a strong or weak or commanding personality. And the usage is instructive as bearing witness to the fact that a man's character represents his whole self. He may be predominantly thoughtful or predominantly wilful or predominantly loving. But his character is not constituted merely by the salient feature, but by the fact that he has chosen to subordinate his other faculties to this one; that he is a thinker who has bent his will and affections into the service of his thought, or a lover who has subdued his thought and will to his love. Or, to put the same thing in another way, the necessity for division of labour makes our ordinary thought and conduct mainly departmental. We specialize ourselves upon a particular science or subsection of a science, or an occupation which may be as limited as the manufacture of one piece of a machine—a wheel, a bolt, a screw. But we only follow these partial pursuits with a view to the ultimate satisfaction of our whole personality: special studies as a step towards the complete unity of knowledge, which can alone satisfy the mind, as we say, meaning the will and desires of the thinker; and manual or other industries, to gain the means of maintaining our life, and the home in which all its interests and instincts may find their scope; while even the departmental work itself will be a failure, unless we put our whole heart into it, making it a moral and emotional as well as a merely mental or mechanical act; whereas, if we do this, the most limited and finite occupation reacts upon and furthers the development of our entire character.

Personality, then, lives and grows, but, in so doing, retains its identity; the character in which it issues, however versatile or complex, being never a disconnected aggregate, but always an organic whole. Its unity may seem to vanish in the variety of experience through which it goes, yet only to reappear, enlarged, enriched, developed, or impoverished and degraded, as the case may be, but self-identical.

We have now said enough in general description of a term that does not admit of being precisely defined. And, in passing on to use it for controversial purposes, we must remember that this incapability of definition is a sign, not of its weakness, but of its strength; being a characteristic of all ultimate realities, just because they are so real—as Locke saw in the case of what he called 'simple ideas.' Every man is certain of his own personality, and has no need to be convinced of it; though not every man has reflected upon it, to see what it implies. But its chief attributes are so obvious that, when once attention has been called to them, they cannot fail to be immediately recognized in their true light. And these, as we have seen, are individuality, self-consciousness, self-determination, love and, as the result of their living interaction, character.

Now personality is the inevitable and necessary starting-point of all human thought. For we cannot by any conceivable means get out of it, or behind it, or beyond it, or account for it, or imagine the method of its derivation from anything else. For, strictly speaking, we have no knowledge of anything else from which it can have been derived. If we are told that it is the product of pure reason, or unconscious will, or mere matter or blind force, the answer is obvious—that we know of no such things. For, when spoken of in this way, reason and will and matter and force are only abstractions, and abstractions from my personal experience; that is to say, they are parts of myself, separated from their context and then supposed to exist in the outer world; or, to put the same thing in another way, they are phenomena of the outer world, which are supposed to resemble parts of myself taken out of their context. But it is only in their context that these parts of me have any real existence. Will, in the only form in which I know it, is determined by reason and desire. Matter, in the only form in which I know it—that is, in my own body—is informed by reason and desire and will. Reason, as I know it, is inseparable from desire and will. And when in my own case I speak of my 'reason' or my 'will' apart, I am making abstraction of a particular aspect of myself, which, as such, has only an ideal or imaginary existence. Consequently, names which are given to phenomena in virtue of their resembling or being supposed to resemble these abstract aspects of myself, must be equally ideal and imaginary in their denotation. And I cannot in any way conceive a living and complex whole, like myself, to be derived from anything outside me which can only be known and named because it resembles one of my elements; when the element in question must be artificially isolated and, so to speak, killed in the process, before the resemblance can be established. Abstractions must be less real than the totality from which they are taken, and cannot thus be made levers for displacing their own fulcrum. Personality, therefore, is ultimate 'a parte ante.'

It follows from this that personality is also our canon of reality[1], the most real thing we know, and by comparison with which we estimate the amount of reality in other things. For, however difficult the notion of reality be to define, we may accept the evidence of language, in itself no mean metaphysician, to the general view that there are degrees of it. 'Quo plus realitatis ... res habet, eo plura attributa ei competunt' is a proposition of Spinoza on which Lotze rightly remarks that its converse is equally true—'The greater the number of attributes that attach to anything, the more real that thing is'[2]; which is equivalent to saying, the greater the number of ways in which it is related to my personality. For example, a fear of ghosts may be a real enough obstacle to prevent a man from traversing a certain path. But a tree blown across it would be a more real obstacle, a wild beast more real, and an armed enemy more real still; because their respective oppositions would affect the man in an increasing

---

[1] See note 8.   [2] Lotze, *Metaphys.* § 49.

number of ways. So a living flower is more real than a dead one, for it has more attributes; but if the dead one was given me by a friend it is the more real of the two to me, because it wakes more echoes in me and touches more of my entire being. For the same reason whatever affects me permanently or intensely is more real than a thing whose relation to me is momentary or slight. And, as nothing influences me so variously or intensely, or possesses so permanent a possibility of influence as another person, personality is the most real thing which I can conceive outside me, since it corresponds most completely to my own personality within. Hence each person is, as we have already seen, an end to me, and not a means to an end; something which in that particular direction I cannot go beyond, and in which I am content to rest; and the world of persons is in consequence more real to me than the world of nature or of books. Nor does this in any degree reduce 'reality' to a merely subjective experience; because the same principle can obviously be, and invariably is, extended to what affects all persons and at all times in a similar way. And, if there is any obscurity in the above statement, it simply arises from the fact that, for the practical purposes of ordinary life, we are content with a more compendious view of reality; ascribing it to whatever possesses two or three of its most prominent attributes, such as persistence and the power of being seen or touched. But, on analysis, this can be shown to be only a convenient abbreviation for the more complete relationship to personality which we have described.

Now the significance of all this is that we are spiritual beings. The word spirit is indeed undefinable and may even be called indefinite, but it is not a merely negative term for the opposite of matter. It has a sufficiently distinct connotation for ordinary use. It implies an order of existence which transcends the order of sensible experience, the material order: yet which, so far from excluding the material order, includes and elevates it to higher use, precisely as the chemical includes and transfigures the mechanical, or the vital the chemical order. It is thus synonymous with supernatural, in the strict sense of the term. And personality as above described belongs to this spiritual order, the only region in which self-consciousness and freedom can have place.

Historically, then, man has always believed himself to be a spiritual being. Here and there at intervals the belief has been reasoned out of him. But there is no question that it represents his normal conviction. It is stereotyped, under one form or another, in every language; it is assumed in his earliest literature; and is implied in the burial customs of even the palaeolithic age. Here, then, is a solid fact, scientifically ascertained. Man believes himself to be spiritual.

Critical analysis justifies the belief. And it should be borne in mind that an analysis which justifies a universal conviction has an immense presumption in its favour, and therefore a cumulative force; while one of an opposite tendency must to a great extent be neutralized, if it cannot after all discredit in the popular mind the conviction which it claims to have explained away. 'E pur se muove.' In the present case, the unity of our self-consciousness, with the further sense of freedom that it involves, is its own evidence. It knows itself to differ, *toto caelo*, from all that we call material. Space and time, for instance, are necessary conditions of material existence, including that of my own material organism. But I am conscious that in knowing things I take them out of space and time, and invest them, so to speak, with an entirely different mode of existence, which has no analogue outside my consciousness. Multiplicity and movement are essential characteristics of the material world, whereas I am conscious of being permanently self-identical and one. Otherwise I could be no more aware of multiplicity and movement than my bodily senses are of the earth's revolution, as they are carried with it in its course. Necessity or determination from without is characteristic of the material world, one event producing another in endless continuity of causation; whereas I am directly conscious of being self-determined from within—a source of original activity, a free agent, a will.

These are not, of course, independent arguments proving my spirituality as their conclusion; for if so regarded they would obviously beg the question. But they are reasons which my self-consciousness sees, on examination, for its own spontaneous verdict about itself. Man lives first, and thinks afterwards. He is implicitly aware of his spirituality; and, when cross-questioned, can only make explicit the evidence which he finds within him for the fact. Materialism, on the other hand, cannot explain away either this time-honoured testimony of consciousness, or the grounds on which it is found to rest. All its attempts to do so are mere efforts of imagination, whether we examine them from the metaphysical or the physical side. For the assertion that what we call spirit is a mode of matter, or derived from matter, must mean from such matter as we know; otherwise it would merely be dealing with the unknown, and have no meaning at all. But matter, as we know it, is always in synthesis with spirit, a synthesis in which each of the two factors acts and reacts upon the other. Objectivity, externality, extension, motion and all such terms imply a subject as their necessary correlative; for to think at all is to relate an object to a subject, and to obliterate the relation is to cease to think. Consequently, to speak of matter, or force, or generally of the objective element in knowledge as existing by itself, or out of relation to a subject, is to speak of it otherwise than as we know it, and to use words without a meaning[1]. Yet this is precisely what the materialist does; and in so doing he is the dupe of his own imagination. He first isolates by abstraction certain elements of his total experience, and calls them 'force' or 'matter'; he then substantiates or solidifies these 'abstract ideas' through his imagination, till they look as if they existed by themselves, and so is able to picture them as creating the mind by which, in fact, they have been created. The same thing may be stated, in a way which is more obvious to many minds, from the physical point of view; and is so stated, with some authority, by Du Bois-Reymond. 'The complete knowledge of the brain,' he says, 'the highest knowledge we can attain, reveals to us nothing but matter in motion.' . . . 'What conceivable connexion exists between certain movements of certain atoms in my brain on the one hand, and on the other the, to me, original and not further definable but undeniable facts, "I feel pain, feel pleasure; I take something sweet, smell roses, hear organ-sounds, see something red," and the just as immediately resulting certainty,

[1] See note 9.

"therefore I am"?... It is impossible to see how from the co-operation of the atoms consciousness can result. Even if I were to attribute consciousness to the atoms, that would neither explain consciousness in general nor would that in any way help us to understand the unitary consciousness of the individual [1].' Lotze[2] further enlarges upon this last point, and disposes of the mechanical analogy which would resolve the unity of consciousness into a resultant of a number of separate forces, by reminding us that in mechanics the various forces in question must act simultaneously upon one and the same material point; so that in the present case the unity which is to be explained will have to be already presupposed. This impassable gulf, then, between matter and thought, which all philosophically minded men of science admit, is another aspect of their inseparable connexion as viewed by the metaphysician. And when Cabanis, and others after him, call thought a secretion of the brain, they merely conceal this gulf under the cloud of an imaginative phrase which, as Fichte says, 'has never conveyed a thought to any man, and never will.' The witness of our consciousness, therefore, to its own spirituality never has been and never can be explained away by materialism. From the physical point of view

---

[1] Qu. by Lange, *Hist. of Mat.* ii. p. 311 (E. T.).
[2] Lotze, *Metaphys.* § 242.

we cannot, of course, say more than that it never has been explained, because physical science cannot go beyond its experience; and if, therefore, the physical point of view were the only one, there might always remain the possibility of an explanation being some day discovered. It is, in fact, upon this possibility that the materialist rests. The process in question is as yet inconceivable, he will admit, in the sense that it cannot be pictured by the mind; but that is merely because as yet we have had no experience of it; we have not gone deep enough into nature's laboratory to see it at work; but meanwhile there are so many analogies in its favour that we may expect its discovery will one day come. If the major premiss of all this could be granted the conclusion would be fair enough. And hence the paramount importance of emphasizing the metaphysical view of the question, which, by exhibiting the necessary limits of all possible experience, can alone convert the 'has not been' into 'cannot be.'

It might indeed be thought that, after all which Kant and his successors have said upon the subject, materialism would be, by this time, a thing of the past. But it is not so. 'Strictly considered,' says Lange, its well-known historian, 'scientific research does not produce Materialism; but neither does it refute it, . . . nevertheless, in actual life and in the daily interchange of opinions, scientific inquiry by no means occupies so neutral or even negative an attitude towards Materialism as is the case when all consequences are rigidly followed out. . . . After all the "confutations" of Materialism, now more than ever, there appear books of popular science and periodical essays which base themselves upon materialistic views as calmly as if the matter had been settled long ago.' These complacent reiterations of an untenable position he goes on to attribute to ignorance of critical philosophy on the part of many scientific specialists. And as no one could accuse Lange of obscurantism his conclusion should carry weight. 'There are only two conditions,' he continues, 'under which this (materialistic) consequence can be avoided. The one lies behind us: it is the *authority of philosophy*, and the deep influence of religion upon men's minds. The other still lies some distance ahead: it is the general spread of *philosophical culture* among all who devote themselves to scientific studies[1].' And until this spread of culture comes, the authority of philosophy, represented as it is by an august catena, reaching from Plato to the present day, should command at least as much respect among the students of science and their uncritical admirers as is willingly conceded by the layman to the expert in all other departments of life and thought. For the authority of philosophy is like

[1] Lange, *Hist. of Mat.* ii. p. 332 (E. T.).

the wisdom of the aged; it does not supersede independent thought, but it supplies guidance and protection to those whose leisure for thought is limited or whose capacity is still immature; while, further, the general agreement of philosophers on any point creates a very strong presumption of its truth. In the present case, it may fairly be maintained that there exists an overwhelming majority of philosophers who, amid many differences, are agreed upon the spiritual character of man. And the object of the above survey has been simply to give prominence to those fundamental points in our personality for which there is at least enough philosophic authority to give the ablest adversaries pause, as well as to indicate the lines of analysis, or of argument, on which they rest.

It should be noticed, in conclusion, that though personality, as above described, is the one thing which we know best in the world, it is also the most mysterious thing we know[1]. 'Grande profundum est homo.' There are 'abysmal deeps of personality' which startle us at times by the vastness of the vistas which they half disclose. We are dimly aware of undeveloped capabilities within us—capabilities of energy, intelligence and love—which we cannot conceive ultimately frustrated and functionless; germs without a future, seeds without a fruit; and which, therefore, irresistibly

[1] See note 10.

point to immortality as the sole condition in which a personal being can find scope. 'In point of fact,' says Lotze—and the quotation will indicate our whole subsequent line of thought—'In point of fact, we have little ground for speaking of the personality of finite beings; it is an ideal and, like all that is ideal, belongs unconditionally only to the Infinite. Perfect personality is in God only; to all finite minds there is allotted but a pale copy thereof; the finiteness of the finite is not a producing condition of this personality, but a limit and hindrance of its development[1].'

[1] Lotze, *Microcosm.* ix. 4, § 4.

LECTURE III

DEVELOPMENT OF THE CONCEPTION OF DIVINE PERSONALITY

MAN'S belief in a personal God, from whatever source it is derived, must obviously be interpreted through his consciousness of his own personality. We should naturally expect to find, therefore, that it has gradually, like the latter, grown articulate from an implicit and unreflective stage. And before we can fairly criticize, or allow it to be criticized, we must be familiar with the steps of its historic evolution. For the inference on which it rests, or by which, at least, it must be justified when called in question, is of that highly complex kind in which a multitude of probable arguments converge and corroborate each other. And foremost among these arguments is the fact of the universality, or at least the extreme generality of the belief, in an elementary form. This is a fact of primary importance, not only for its intrinsic value as an argument, but for the light which it throws upon all subsequent arguments, by showing that they are not to be regarded as the premisses of a conclusion, but as the analytical explanations of a pre-established conviction. As we live first and think afterwards, so we are religious first and theological afterwards. Our religion anticipates all argument. And it may be remarked in passing that this effectively disposes of the superficial objections which are often urged against the evidences of religion, on the ground of their subtle and complex character; for these evidences are plainly seen, in the light of history, to be afterthoughts—ways of explaining, but not of attaining, religious life.

'The statement,' says Tiele, 'that there are nations or tribes which possess no religion rests either on inaccurate observation or on a confusion of ideas. No tribe or nation has yet been met with, destitute of belief in any higher beings; and travellers who asserted their existence have been afterwards refuted by the facts. It is legitimate, therefore, to call religion in its most general sense an universal phenomenon of humanity[1].' Tylor fully endorses this view; while De Quatrefages, approaching the subject from a totally different direction, as a naturalist, is equally emphatic: 'We nowhere meet,' he says, 'with atheism, except in an *erratic condition*. In every place, and at all times, the mass of populations have escaped it; we

[1] *Outlines of H. of R.* i. 6 (E. T.).

nowhere find either a great human race, or even a division, however unimportant, of that race, professing atheism ... A belief in beings superior to man, and capable of exercising a good or evil influence upon his destiny; and the conviction that the existence of man is not limited to the present life, but that there remains for him a future beyond the grave. . . . . every people, every man believing these two things is *religious*, and observation shows more and more clearly every day the universality of this character [1].'

Whether or not the beliefs of modern savages are the nearest analogue of primitive religion is, from the scientific point of view, an open question. We must remember that moral and religious degeneracy is undoubtedly a *vera causa*, a process that has operated widely and deeply in human history; and that modern savages may, therefore, have declined from a once higher level. Still there is tolerably clear evidence that the religious belief of our race has passed through a stage which, if short of the extreme of savagery, was very rudimentary. Of course this may have been preceded by a primitive monotheism, and there are distinguished specialists who still maintain that the earlier forms of Egyptian and Indian religion were more monotheistic than the later. But the general tendency of the evidence is the other way,

[1] Quatrefages, *Human Species*, p. 482.

and seems to point to a very gradual awakening of the religious consciousness, though by no means through such a definite series of stages as some systematizers would have us suppose. Fetichism, Totemism, Atavism, Polydaemonism, Polytheism, Henotheism cannot really be arranged in a serial order; nor need we now pause upon the attempts made so to arrange them. For our present purpose it is sufficient to notice the primitive philosophy which underlies them all—that is, animism. Animism is the belief in souls or spirits animating the external world, the first and most obvious method of accounting for its various phenomena. It is not in itself a religion, but in alliance with the religious instinct gives birth to various forms of religion according to the variety of objects in which spirits are supposed to dwell—stones, trees, beasts, winds, rivers, mountains, stars—being all in their turn conceived of as the homes or bodies of spiritual agents; and this by no 'pathetic fallacy' or poetic transference of attributes, but by an intellectual necessity. Man's only certain knowledge was of himself, and he was obliged to interpret the outside world, therefore, in terms of that self, while language in its earlier stages inevitably carried on the process.

'We always find the myth-constructing beginnings of religion busied in transforming natural to spiritual reality, but never find them actuated by any desire to trace back living spiritual activity to unintelligent Realness as a firmer foundation [1].'

'Whatever had to be called and conceived had to be conceived as active, had to be called by means of roots which expressed originally the consciousness of our own acts [2].'

Personification, then, was the beginning of philosophy and theology alike, and that by a psychological necessity; for in all thinking we work from the known to the unknown, and the 'known' to primitive man was himself. But we have already seen that uncivilized man has a very dim and obscure sense both of the limits and the content of his own personality: his morality is limited, his character impulsive, the elements of his nature loosely coherent, and not yet welded together into unity. And all this was naturally reflected in his view of the outside world, with the result that his gods were indefinite in number and in outline, and their character 'vengeful, partial, passionate, unjust.' But as time went on, and man learned to distinguish between animate and inanimate, persons and things, and again between what was essential and accidental, good and bad in his own nature, higher conceptions of divine personality and character arose; culminating in what has been called Henotheism, or monarchical polytheism—that is, in a

---

[1] Lotze, *Microcosm*. ix. 4, § 3.
[2] Max Müller, *Nat. Religion*, p. 390.

polytheism of which some one chief member, like Varuna or Indra, Zeus or Apollo, Woden or Thor, assumes such prominence in a given period or neighbourhood as to overshadow all his compeers and virtually initiate a monotheism. 'For the slumbering faith in a highest God might,' as Grimm says, 'wake up at any moment'; and

> 'The beings so contrarious that seemed gods,
> Prove just His operation manifold
> And multiform, translated, as must be,
> Into intelligible shape so far
> As suits our sense and sets us free to feel[1].'

This purifying process of criticism is fully exhibited in Plato and the Greek tragedians, and with an intenser accompaniment of moral indignation in the Hebrew prophets; and there are traces of it to be found in all religious literature—efforts to

> 'Correct the portrait by the living face,
> Man's God by God's God in the mind of man[1].'

while, as worthier conceptions of God came to be entertained, they in turn reacted upon and raised the standard of human character, and thereby prepared the way for their own further purification, yet still under the form of personality.

The process thus summarized is a long one, and modern anthropology has made its details so familiar to us that they need not be repeated. But its significance is often misrepresented. It

[1] Browning, *Ring and Book*.

is often supposed that the early tendency to personification was gradually outgrown with the growth of enlightenment. But this is not the case; it was only rectified. Man finds the world outside him to be intensely, unquestionably real. It warms, cheers, supports, sustains, helps, hinders, obstructs, hurts, terrifies, destroys him. And he personifies it because it is so real, and personality is, as we have already seen, his supreme canon of reality. These external influences which so affect him are not less real than himself; therefore they must be personal. Consequently, when on further reflection he finds that his immediate environment is largely impersonal, he only relegates personality to the background, without ceasing to regard it as the source of reality. His own personality acts daily through inanimate instruments—the mill, the hammer, the arrow, the spear; and he has no difficulty in conceiving a similar process to be at work in the outer world. Thus, however much the conceptions of them may be rectified and refined, the God or gods of the religious consciousness remain ultimately personal. But there comes a time when the religious consciousness demands intellectual justification; and this demand may arise either from the scientific or the speculative side. As the processes of physical nature come to be better understood, their apparent independence of all spiritual influence may suggest the thought, that perhaps after all there is no such thing as a personality behind them. On the other hand, the contrast between God and man may seem so complete as entirely to preclude the possibility of including both under a common predicate or, in other words, of knowing God at all. We have ample evidence of this stage of development in ancient India and elsewhere; but it is nowhere so compactly summarized, so adequately examined, or so essentially related to ourselves, as in the history of Greek philosophy—the lineal ancestor of all European and Western thought. Greek philosophy begins with the distinct, though naturally crude expression of both the above-mentioned tendencies of thought—the physical speculations of the Ionians and Atomists rendering a God superfluous, and the metaphysical and logical reasoning of the Eleatics declaring Him to be unknowable, as having no resemblance to humanity either in body or in mind; so that we can only conjecture about Him, whether we say 'Him' or 'It.' Matthew Arnold has applied the term 'modern' to Greek civilization; and nothing can be more 'modern' than the pre-Socratic expression of the negative stage in philosophic thought. It is significant, therefore, to notice the historical position of this negative stage. It was the naïve beginning, not the mature end, of Greek speculation, and led inevitably to the more positive and constructive work of Plato and of Aristotle.

The precise theology of Plato and Aristotle is exceedingly difficult to define; and the problem has been rendered harder, by the fact that so many subsequent philosophers have appropriated their doctrines, and unconsciously modified them in the process. But this difficulty must not be exaggerated, and lies rather in their details than their principles. The complete conception of a personal God, in our sense, they did not, and probably could not reach, for the simple reason that they had not, as we have seen, a clear conception of human personality. But we find in them the essential elements of such a conception, and elements so treated as almost to necessitate their subsequent development in this direction—'scattered fragments asking to be combined.' Plato, as is well known, regards the world as an embodiment of eternal, architypal ideas which, though reached in human knowledge by a process of abstraction, are in themselves more substantially real than any of their partial and therefore perishable manifestations in the world of sense. Living in an age whose forms of thought must have been largely influenced by its plastic art, he speaks at first of these ideas as immutable, stationary types. But later on—and he lived to be old—he conceives these ideas to have energy and movement, and relationship one with another. Further, he groups these ideas under one supreme central idea, variously described as the Good, or the idea of Good, or Goodness Itself, which, he says, is the cause of all things right and fair, of light and its parent, of truth and of reason, and which is in one place identified with divine reason, and possibly in another with the divine beauty. This ideal theory is his philosophic answer to materialism, and is deduced from the evidence of reason, goodness, and beauty in the world. But side by side with it he uses the ordinary religious language of his day, speaking dogmatically of God and the gods, without any attempt at their demonstration. And in the *Timaeus*, the treatise with which Raphael paints him, but which has since been too much neglected, he speaks of the Maker and Father of the universe, whom it is hard to discover and still harder to describe, as fashioning the world in imitation of an eternal pattern—and that because he was good and in him was no envy at all. Now Plato's whole religious tone is too earnest and enthusiastic to allow for a moment of our regarding this theological way of speaking as a mere accommodation to the popular mind, a mythical presentation of abstract thought. Nor is there any trace in him of the later distinction between philosophic and religious truth (veritas secundum fidem, and veritas secundum philosophiam), which is only a disguise for unbelief in one or other of the two. Consequently, we must suppose that he either identified the idea of Good with the personal God, or that he viewed both conceptions as true, without seeing how they should be reconciled. In either case he substantially teaches the personality of God, for which we must remember there was as yet no precise terminology existing; and in the latter he is on the verge of the profounder doctrine of eternal distinctions in the Godhead, for which he unquestionably, as a fact of history, paved the way.

Aristotle exhibits far less religious feeling than Plato; but his theology is more scientifically worked out, and not without traces of a suppressed enthusiasm which has been compared to that of Bishop Butler. He criticizes Plato for separating his ideas so completely from the material world, and himself regards the ideas or rational principles of things as immanent in nature, like the order in an army, while only the highest idea is wholly immaterial, and exists apart, like the general of an army. This highest idea or form is God, who is pure reason, and whose eternal and continuous activity consists in contemplative thought. And as this reason can have no adequate object outside itself, it must be its own object and contemplate itself. Hence the divine life consists in self-contemplation. And though God, therefore, does not actively influence the world, He is the cause of all its life and move-

ment, as being the universal object of desire—
'Himself unmoved, all motion's source.' Plato
bridges the intellectual gaps in his system by his
enthusiastic faith; and for want of this the Aristotelian theology is more obviously defective; but
it represents a distinct advance in thinking, and,
further, leaves the subject in a form which almost
necessitates its subsequent development. Plato
and Aristotle were succeeded by an age of philoso-
phizing, but not of philosophers, an age of archae-
ological revivals in thought, in which much was
done to popularize, but little to advance speculation, except in an ethical direction. For our present
purpose they stand alone, and their significance is
this: they answered materialism and agnosticism,
as far as it had then appeared, on the ground that
the world exhibits a rational order, and must, therefore, have a rational cause; and this was really
a more important contribution to theology than the
fact, that probably the former, and possibly the
latter of them regarded this rational cause as what
we should now call personal. But, before the
conception of divine personality could be more
adequately developed, another influence was needed,
and one with truer and deeper ethical insight than
the Greek. The Hebrew prophets, from Moses
onwards, with their superior hold upon morality,
which is the very nerve of personality, purified
their popular religion, but without losing them-

F

selves in abstractions; and it is a mere travesty of criticism to speak of their God as an impersonal tendency. From beginning to end He is essentially personal. And to whatever extent Persian influence affected later Jewish thought, and thereby flowed into the general history of the world, it must have been to the same effect. For the religion of the Avesta comes nearest to the Hebrew, both in its intense sense of righteousness, and its consequent conviction of a righteous and therefore a Personal God. Now the Christian conception of God was, of course, the legitimate and lineal descendant of the Hebrew; it took up, that is, the religious tradition of humanity, in the purest form which it had yet attained. It came from the side of religion and not of philosophy. But the belief in the Incarnation, while it intensified and emphasized the notion of divine personality, necessitated a further intellectual analysis of what that notion meant, and issued in the doctrine of the Trinity in Unity—a doctrine which, plainly implied, as we believe it to be, in the New Testament and earlier fathers of the Church, did not attain its finally explicit formulation till the fourth century. And in this process Greek philosophy played an important part. We may now dismiss as wholly untenable the notion that the doctrine of the Trinity was borrowed either from Plato or any other ethnic source. It was implicit in the Christian creed.

That creed could not be thought out without reaching it. And it became explicit in the Christian consciousness, under the double necessity for explaining the creed to philosophic minds, and defending its integrity against philosophic opposition. But the men who conducted the process of this development were trained in the philosophy of Alexandria and Athens. Their language and its connotation, their categories, their modes of thought were Greek. The facts on which they worked, the material they had to fashion was Christian. But the instrument with which they fashioned it, and the skill to use the instrument, had come to them from Plato, Aristotle, Zeno and their schools. And we may fairly say that Greek philosophy only reached its goal when it thus passed, under Christian influence, into the service of a Personal God. And in this sense the doctrine of the Trinity was the synthesis, and summary, of all that was highest in the Hebrew and Hellenic conceptions of God, fused into union by the electric touch of the Incarnation.

Now the doctrine of the Trinity, as dogmatically elaborated, is, in fact, the most philosophical attempt to conceive of God as Personal. Not that it arose from any mere processes of thinking. These, as we have seen, all stopped short of it. It was suggested by the Incarnation, considered as a new revelation about God, and thought out upon the lines indicated in the New Testament. Upon this the evidence of the Fathers is plain. They felt that they were in presence of a fact which, so far from being the creation of any theory of the day, was a mystery— a thing which could be apprehended when revealed, but could neither be comprehended nor discovered; and their reasoning upon the subject is always qualified by a profound sense of this mysteriousness. Athanasius often figures in popular controversy as the typical dogmatist. Yet it is Athanasius who says, 'Nor must we ask why the Word of God is not such as our word, considering God is not such as we, as has been before said; nor, again, is it right to seek how the Word is from God, or how He is God's radiance, or how God begets, and what is the manner of His begetting. For a man must be beside himself to venture on such points: since a thing ineffable and proper to God's nature, and known to Him alone and to the Son, this he demands to have explained in words. It is all one as if they sought where God is, and how God is, and of what nature the Father is. But as to ask such questions is impious, and argues an ignorance of God, so it is not permitted to venture such questions concerning the generation of the Son of God, nor to measure God and His wisdom by our own nature and infirmity[1].' Such passages might be multiplied indefinitely; and St. John of Damascus,

---

[1] *Orat. c. Arian.* ii. § 56 (Newman's trans.).

who on many points sums up the Patristic teaching, says, 'What God is is incomprehensible and unknowable[1].' Now this language, which was afterwards developed into the negative theology (via negationis) of pseudo-Dionysius, Erigena, and the mystics, and which led the Fathers to protest against the Gnostics, Arians and Sabellians, for rationalizing mysteries, shows a thorough consciousness of the true element in Agnosticism; and teachers who thus carefully qualify their statements cannot certainly be accused of undue anthropomorphism. But, on the other hand, they lay much stress on the thought of man's being created in the image of God, and upon the illuminating presence of the Spirit of God in the Christian intellect, at times even describing His operation as 'deifying.' And, starting from these premisses, they freely apply human analogies to illustrate the doctrine of the Trinity.

If we recur to our previous analysis of human personality we shall see that it is essentially triune, not because its chief functions are three—thought, desire, and will—for they might perhaps conceivably be more, but because it consists of a subject, an object, and their relation. A person is, as we have seen, a subject who can become an object to himself, and the relation of these two terms is necessarily a third term. I cannot think, or desire, or will,

---

[1] *De Fid. Orth.* i. 4.   [2] See note 11.

without an object, which is either simply myself, or something associated with myself, or dissociated from myself considered as an object, in either case involving my objectivity to myself. When I say '*I* think this,' '*I* like that,' '*I* will do the other,' I am considering myself as an object quite as much as 'this,' 'that' and 'the other.' And I cannot think of the world I live in, without thinking of it negatively as outside *me*, or positively as including *me*, in either case related to myself. We may ignore this association for practical purposes, or we may be entirely unconscious of it, but on analysis it can always be detected. And it is through this power of becoming an object to myself that all my subsequent knowledge is attained. However various and extended my objective world may become, it is still one object in relation to me; and however complex my relations to it, they are still my own, or one totality of relationship to that object. And thus my personality is essentially and necessarily triune. Further, we have seen that our personality is at first a mere potentiality, which gradually develops or realizes itself, and that in this process of realization it seeks association with other persons. It needs to include other persons within the sphere of its own objectivity, to fill, so to say, its blank form of objectivity with personal objects, its blank form of relationship with personal relations. And the first shape which this association takes is the family, the unit of society. The family is the first stage in the development and completion of our personality; its abstract triunity being therein adequately, because personally, realized in father, mother, and child.

Of course this concrete social trinity is much more obvious than its psychological counterpart and cause, and could not fail from an early period to mould men's forms of thought. Hence we find the gods of polytheism continually grouped in triads, sometimes as triumvirates, sometimes as families—especially in India and Egypt—a fact which would naturally familiarize men's minds with trinitarian modes of thinking in theology. But as the sense of human personality grew deeper, particularly, as we have seen, under Christian influence, its triune character was gradually recognized. Augustine marks an epoch in the subject and is its best exponent. 'I exist,' he says, 'and I am conscious that I exist, and I love the existence and the consciousness; and all this independently of any external influence.' And again, 'I exist, I am conscious, I will. I exist as conscious and willing, I am conscious of existing and willing, I will to exist and to be conscious; and these three functions, though distinct, are inseparable and form one life, one mind, one essence.' Neo-Platonism is full of kindred thoughts; but they were implicit in the philosophic and religious consciousness long before Augustine or the Neo-Platonists. And though Trinitarian formulae were explicitly employed in theology sooner than in psychology, applied to God sooner than to man, it was, of course, from the latter that they were really derived. The instrument was, in fact, being fashioned in the using; and human personality was coming gradually to a clearer conception of itself, by the very act of using its own processes to illustrate the doctrine of the Trinity.

Now the doctrine of the Trinity is often crudely attacked, as being simply derived from the analogy of the family, which, as we have seen, played an important part in pre-Christian mythology and theology. It should be remembered, therefore, that since the family is an essential outcome of our personality under its present conditions of existence, this attack is only a restatement of the general objection against arguing from our personality at all —that is, against using what we have seen to be the only argument that we possess. But, as a matter of fact, the Christian Church did not press the family analogy, at any rate further than the doctrine of the Son. It probably saw early exhibited, among the Gnostic sects, the dangerous practical consequences which might ensue, from the introduction of a feminine principle into our thoughts about the Godhead; and therefore, while freely admitting feminine attributes, declined all thought of a feminine hypostasis, though possibly this may have involved some underestimate of an aspect of truth, which avenged itself in the subsequent development of Mariolatry. It is, therefore, under the more fundamental psychological analogy that we find the doctrine of the Trinity slowly defined, with the natural consequence that the conception of the Word is completed sooner than that of the Spirit, since a personal object is easier to imagine than a personal relation. For the former conception the ground had been prepared, by the Platonic ideas, the Aristotelian view of God as His own necessary object, the seminal reason of the Stoics, the Apocryphal Wisdom, the Philonian Word—all obviously due to psychological analysis. And it was a comparatively easy transition from these to the Christian Logos, who is both 'immanent and eminent' (Theophylus), 'ideal and actual' (Athenagoras), 'a living though immaterial personality, as contrasted with the abstract images of human thought' (Origen), 'the reason and intelligence that is God's counsellor' (Theophylact), 'and shares the solitude of God' (Tertullian), and to which Irenaeus, with his dread of speculation, says men are too ready to apply analogies drawn from the processes of human thought. But for the doctrine of the Spirit, there had been but little, if any, speculative preparation, and its development was proportionately tentative and slow. St. Augustine, very possibly influenced by some hints of the Neo-Platonic Victorinus, is the first to draw out the thought of the Holy Spirit as the bond of union, the coeternal Love, which unites the Father and the Son, thus preparing the way for the acceptance of the double procession, and for the specific designation of the Holy Ghost as Love (St. Thomas). Now all this was an attempt to make the divine nature, and life, to a certain extent intelligible. The Unitarian imagines his conception of God, as an undifferentiated unity, to be simpler than the Christian. But it cannot really be translated into thought. It cannot be thought out. Whereas the Christian doctrine, however mysterious, moves in the direction, at least, of conceivability, for the simple reason that it is the very thing towards which our own personality points. Our own personality is triune; but it is a potential, unrealized triunity, which is incomplete in itself, and must go beyond itself for completion, as, for example, in the family. If, therefore, we are to think of God as personal, it must be by what is called the method of eminence (via eminentiae)—the method, that is, which considers God as possessing, in transcendent perfection, the same attributes which are imperfectly possessed by man[1]. He must, therefore, be pictured as One whose triunity has nothing potential or unrealized about it; whose triune elements are eternally actualized, by no outward influence, but from within; a Trinity in

---

[1] See note 12.

Unity; a social God, with all the conditions of personal existence internal to Himself.

Our present purpose is not to consider the doctrine of the Trinity as a reasonable revelation, for we are not now dealing with revelation at all, but simply to point out the fact that Christianity, which claimed to be the fulfilment of all that was true in previous religion, announced a doctrine of God, which was only intelligible in the light of the analogy drawn from our consciousness of our own personality, and which was dogmatically defined by the assistance of that analogy; and thus emphatically reaffirmed the verdict of man's primitive personifying instinct.

Looking back, then, upon history, we may say that a tendency to believe in divine personality (including polytheism as well as monotheism under the phrase) has been practically universal amongst the human race; that, among other influences, Greek philosophy, and Hebrew prophecy, the one working chiefly from the intellectual, the other from the moral side, strove to eliminate from this belief all that was unworthily anthropomorphic; while in so doing the latter consciously, and the former implicitly, retained the essential attributes of personality, till finally the Christian Church united and developed their results, in the dogma of the Trinity in Unity; which, however much it transcends intelligence, distinctly claims to be the most intelligible mode of conceiving God as essentially personal.

Turning, then, from history to apology, we start from the fact that our belief in a Personal God is founded on an instinctive tendency, morally and philosophically developed. It cannot be called simply either an intuition or an instinct, for it has neither the clearness of the one nor the unerring action of the other, and it is best, therefore, described as an instinctive tendency. Man has an instinctive tendency to believe in a God or gods. And it is this instinctive basis which gives its true character to our theology. Theology was no conscious invention, some of whose results have in the course of time become intuitive, but an attempt to unfold the significance of an already existing intuition or instinct. Men first felt themselves, even if vaguely, to be living in the presence of a God or gods, and afterwards came to reflect upon the nature and consequences of that relation. This fact is of primary importance for the theistic argument, for it at once puts Theism in possession of the field, and throws the *onus probandi* upon its opponents. When we leave the conjectures of hypothetical anthropology, and confine ourselves strictly to what historic science has observed, we find that man has always and everywhere tended to a religious belief. That is a fact of experience scientifically ascertained, and, in founding the external evidences of our faith on it, we claim to build upon a solid foundation of fact. But we are at once met by the attempt to explain away this belief, as a natural delusion, due to the misinterpretation of dreams, to meteorological ignorance, to the dread of animals, or the love of ancestors, or a complex interaction of these various causes.

Now we may fully admit, that these various influences affect uncivilized man to a very considerable degree, and yet reasonably deny their adequacy to produce the persistent, irresistible, practically universal belief in question. The impotence of philosophy to create a religion is a commonplace. Is it likely that savage philosophy succeeded, and that completely and for ever, in a work which civilized philosophy has been notoriously unable to accomplish? And yet it is precisely this that we are asked to believe. To which we answer that it is a very doubtful, and wholly unverified, hypothesis. And it is no reply to accumulate instances of these savage delusions. We neither doubt their existence, nor their influence on early thought, but only their causal connexion with the origin of religion.

But many of us are quite willing to go further than this, and grant that the phenomena of dreams, and storms, and sunshine, and animal activity, were the agencies, through which man's spiritual sense was first consciously awakened, the first objects on which, infant-like, it tentatively fixed; without in any way thereby compromising the authenticity and authority of such a sense. It would seem to be a necessity of human progress, that man should regard the immediate objects of his apprehension, or pursuit, as ends in themselves, ultimate ends; whereas, in fact, when once attained they turn out to be only relative ends, means to other objects, greater and grander than themselves, and, by contrast with those greater things, unreal. Hence, as has been often pointed out, man is always educated by illusions [1].

Now since this principle of development through illusion is thus a natural necessity, and pervades even the most civilized life, we should expect it to operate more powerfully still among ignorant and uncultured races. The method of evolution need not discredit the result evolved. And the feeling after God need be no less veracious a guide, for having first sought to find Him among the objects of His creation—sun, moon, stars, tempests, memories of the beloved dead.

But illusion of this kind is utterly distinct from delusion. An illusion is an inadequate conception; a delusion is a false one. And we may reasonably argue that, if the sense in question was evolved at all, it must have followed the universal law of evolution, and survived because it corresponded

[1] See note 13.

with its environment, or, in other words, was founded on fact, and was therefore not a delusion. The strictly animal instincts have been perfected, and their possessors selected for survival, in exact proportion to the accuracy with which they were adjusted to external fact. 'Can we believe,' it has been well asked, that 'at one point in the process of evolution (and that, mark, at the dawn of the very faculty which is now enabling us to criticize and explore the distortions which follow) that faculty suddenly goes wrong, not specifically in the moral, but in the more general mental sense, and its whole idea-world becomes untrustworthy[1]?' Yet nothing less than this is involved in the attempt to explain the spiritual instinct as a delusion; an alternative which becomes impossible almost to absurdity, when we remember the part which religion has played in the development of our race. When we have eliminated the evil done in the name of religion, which its opponents are somewhat too ready to identify with religion itself, the fact remains that religion has been the chief factor in the higher education of our race. No consistent evolutionist, therefore, can maintain that it is the outcome of an instinct, which never from the first had any real correspondence with external fact, and was untrue. Such paradoxes were common in the eighteenth century, with its tendency to base all

[1] Lady Welby, Brit. Assoc., 1890.

historic institutions upon fictions, but in the present day they are merely survivals of an obsolete philosophy, which our science of historic evolution has conclusively and finally exposed. Indeed, when we consider the weight of the superstructure which man's religious instinct has borne, it becomes difficult to discuss with seriousness, for all their ingenuity, these attempts to explain it away. It remains, as it has ever been, the firm foundation of our belief in a Personal God.

In proceeding to examine the intellectual justification of this belief, we must remember that the instinctive nature of its origin reappears at every stage of its development. It is not, it never has been, a merely intellectual thing; for it is the outcome of our entire personality acting as a whole. Our reason, our affections, our actions, all alike, feel about for contact with some supreme reality; and when the mind, speaking for its companion faculties, names that reality a Person, it is giving voice also to the inarticulate conviction of the heart and will—an instinctive mystical conviction that is, in truth, 'too deep for words.' 'For the heart,' in Pascal's language, 'has reasons of its own, which the reason does not know.'

LECTURE IV

ANALYSIS OF THE CONCEPTION OF DIVINE PERSONALITY

OUR belief in a Personal God is, as we have seen, based upon an instinct, or instinctive judgement, whose universal or practically universal existence is a fact of historical experience, and which we do not find that adverse criticism is adequate to explain away. Consequently, when we come to consider the various evidences, arguments, proofs[1] by which this belief is commonly supported, we must remember that these are all attempts to account for, and explain, and justify something which already exists[2]; to decompose a highly complex, though immediate, judgement into its constituent elements, none of which when isolated can have the completeness or the cogency of the original conviction taken as a whole. 'The truth of our religion, like the truth of common matters,' says Bishop Butler, 'is to be judged by the whole evidence taken together; for probable

[1] See note 14.   [2] See note 15.

proofs, by being added, not only increase the evidence but multiply it[1]'—a thought which is insisted upon at great length by Dr. Newman. 'Formal logical sequence,' he says, 'is not in fact the method by which we are enabled to become certain of what is concrete. . . . The real and necessary method . . . is the cumulation of probabilities, independent of each other, arising out of the nature and circumstances of the particular case which is under review—probabilities too fine to avail separately, too subtle and circuitous to be convertible into syllogisms, too numerous and various for such conversion, even were they convertible.' 'Thought is too keen and manifold, its sources are too remote and hidden, its path too personal, delicate and circuitous, its subject-matter too various and intricate to admit of the trammels of any language, of whatever subtlety and whatever compass[2].' Bacon had the same idea before him, though in another context, when he said, 'The subtlety of nature far surpasses that of the senses or the intellect'; and again, 'Syllogistic reasoning is utterly inadequate to the subtlety of nature[3].' Now, nowhere will all this be so true as in the study of a person. We have already seen that our own personality is a synthesis, an organic unity of attributes, faculties, functions, which presuppose

[1] *Analogy.*   [2] *Grammar of Assent,* pp. 277, 281.
[3] *Novum Organon.*

and involve and qualify each other, and never exist or operate apart; and this may suggest to us how inadequate all argumentative proof must be of the existence, or the nature, or the attributes of a Personal God.

There are a certain number of recognized proofs or lines of argument upon the question, which have been differently emphasized in different ages, and by different classes of mind, but none of which can be said to have lost general credit before the time of Kant. And Kant has been compared by Heine, in a shallow moment, to Robespierre, on the ground that he disproved Theism, as completely as the latter abolished royalty, by finally disposing of these time-honoured proofs. No one, of course, would now endorse such a comparison; but it is worth noting for its forcible expression of the extreme view which might be taken of the negative aspect of Kant's work. For Kant confessedly created an epoch in apology by showing, at least more exhaustively than had ever been done before, the entire inadequacy of the purely intellectual arguments for Theism, considered as attempts at logical demonstration. But he admitted the need of retaining, as an idea of the reason or working hypothesis for thought, this very conception, which could not be logically proved; and, further, subordinated the intellectual to the moral arguments, by which he was himself convinced. Moreover, negations in thought are never final; they are only stages leading on to some new form of affirmation. The persistence of a belief, whose argumentative supports have been removed, is an additional evidence of its inherent strength; and in the case before us the critical modification of its so-called evidences has led to a fuller recognition of the implicit necessity of our belief in a Personal God. 'For these proofs,' as Dr. John Caird says, '... are simply expressions of that impossibility of resting in the finite and of that implicit reference to an Infinite and Absolute mind... seen to be involved in our nature as rational and spiritual beings. Considered as proofs, in the ordinary sense of the word, they are open to the objections which have been frequently urged against them; but viewed as an analysis of the unconscious or implicit logic of religion, as tracing the steps of the process by which the human spirit rises to the knowledge of God, and finds therein the fulfilment of its own highest nature, these proofs possess great value [1].'

First, there is the cosmological argument [2], or argument from the contingency of the world. This may be stated in various ways, but is, perhaps, most popularly known as the argument for a First Cause. Man cannot rest content with the mere spectacle of things, or procession of events, without

[1] Introduction to *Philos. of Religion*, p. 133.   [2] See note 16.

wanting to know how they were made, and why they happen, or, in other words, their cause. And this instinctive craving for a cause is as active in the savage as the sage, being a necessary form of human thought, a way in which we are compelled to think by our very mental constitution. In primitive ages men tend to satisfy this instinct, by attributing natural phenomena to the immediate action of personal beings like themselves—spirits of the air, and the woods, and the waters, smiling through the sunrise, and frowning in the storm. And it is the usual thing to say that the progress of knowledge has consisted in the substitution of natural for personal agencies, of scientific fact for mythological fancy; so that, for instance, we no longer regard thunder as the voice of God, or stormclouds as His armies, or lightnings as His arrows, but as necessary results of an electrical disturbance, which in its turn is due to previous atmospheric conditions, that in their turn can be traced still further back in endless causal sequence. Now, of course it is perfectly true that science has effected this change of view, and owes the whole of its progressive existence to the fact. But we beg a very large question, if we describe this change as a *substitution* of material for spiritual causation, rather than an *interpolation* of stages, or secondary causes, between an effect and its first cause. For scientific or secondary causes, are not causes at all, of the kind which our causal instinct demands; and, though it is the continuous pressure of the causal instinct which has led to their discovery, they only postpone but do not satisfy its need. For secondary causes are only antecedents, or previous states, of the phenomenon in question, pointing us back to more remote antecedents, or previous states: they have been sometimes called the 'sum of the conditions' of the phenomenon, which is obviously only another name for the phenomenon itself. Thus they call for explanation as much as the thing which they profess to explain, and are not answers but only extensions and enlargements of the original question. For the original demands of the causal instinct is, for a first cause, in the sense of something which shall account for the given effect without needing itself to be accounted for; something which is not moved from without, and is consequently self-moved or self-determined from within. Now we have a real though limited experience of such a cause within ourselves, and there alone. We are conscious of being able to originate action, to initiate events, even in a measure to modify the processes of nature, in virtue of our free-will or power of self-determination. 'We are,' as Zeller says, 'the only cause of whose mode of action we have immediate knowledge through inner intuition.' And what we demand, therefore, in a first cause is analogous to what we find within ourselves and nowhere else. Thus primitive man, however unscientific, was not altogether unphilosophical. Being ignorant of the world's organic unity, he assumed for it a plurality of personal causes, and as a natural consequence confused what we now call first and secondary causation—that is, the immediate action of personality with the means through which it acts. But, though subsequent science has corrected both these errors—and in so doing has been often thought to relegate personality into the background—it has not affected, and cannot affect, our demand for a personal first cause. If we pick a flower, and ask ourselves how it came into existence, to be told that it has been in making for a million ages, and once existed as nebular dust, enormously increases the interest of our question, but in no way supplies us with its answer. A vast history is unrolled before us, of which the flower is an inseparable part; but we are obliged by our causal instinct to view the whole of this as one effect, and to ask what was its ultimate or uncaused cause. And this brings us to the common objection, that a first cause, and an infinite series of antecedents, or secondary causes, are equally inconceivable; or, as it is sometimes stated, that a first cause is a mere negation of thought, a mere result of our inability to go on thinking indefinitely backward—the point at which we stop in our impotence, but which involves no positive idea. It will follow from what has gone before that this is a mistake. An infinite series of antecedents is not only inconceivable, in the sense that it cannot be pictured by the mind— it is actually unthinkable, for it violates the very nature of thought, which is to demand a cause that shall have no antecedent. Whereas a first cause, in the sense of a self-moved mover, has been recognized by philosophers, from Plato to Hegel, as a positive notion, not an impotence of thought, and is illustrated by the analogy of our personal self-determination, the thing of all others in the whole world which we know best. The case stands, therefore, thus: we are, by universal admission, obliged to think a first cause; we have ample authority for asserting the thought to convey a positive meaning; and we can only interpret that meaning as involving personality. It is, perhaps, unfortunate, that we should have to use the word 'first' at all in this connexion; for a 'first' cause easily suggests the earliest member of a series, and thus gives colour to the above-mentioned fallacy; whereas the cause in question is not merely *a* first cause but *the* first cause—wholly different, that is, in kind from others—supreme, independent, unique; the only cause which our causal instinct can recognize as such; the necessary correlative of any and every effect; so that we cannot think of anything as an effect, or derived mode of being, without necessarily thinking of its original, underived cause. This cause may or may not act through an intermediate series of agents; but the thought of it is as immediately presented to the mind, when we pick a daisy, as when we contemplate the ageless evolution of the stars. The same argument may be otherwise presented, as from relative to absolute, or finite to infinite being. The empirical school maintain that we have no positive conception of the infinite. The infinite, they say, can only mean the indefinite, the et-cetera beyond the finite, which merely serves to symbolize our inability to go on thinking any further—as when the savage counts 'one,' 'two,' 'three,' 'a great many': and, moreover, as the infinite is the negation of the finite, it must obviously be limited by the finite, and cannot, therefore, be infinite at all. This would be all very plausible if the finite and the infinite were only different in quantity, and not in quality or kind; if, in short, they were mere abstractions from which all but quantity had been taken away. But this is not, in fact, the meaning of the terms as employed in the argument with which we are concerned. For when we speak of inferring the infinite from the finite, this finite, from which our reasoning starts, is no abstraction, but the real, visible, substantial, concrete world around us, quick with all its palpitating life. Consequently, when we argue that this finite implies an infinite, we do not mean that it implies an abstract fringe of emptiness outside it; but, on the contrary, that it implies something infinitely more comprehensive, and concrete than itself, something which underlies, and includes, and sustains it, an infinite reality, an infinite fulness, a totality of which it is a part. For finite objects are unstable and have no permanent identity; indeed, in a sense they have no identity at all, since they are determined by, and therefore dependent on other finite objects, situations, surroundings, atmospheres, contexts and the like; all of which are incessantly changing and involving others in their change. Water evaporates, air is decomposed, plants and animals die daily, and are resolved into their dust: everything is in process of becoming something other than itself. Yet all the while we regard the world as real, and substantial, and recognize a method and a system in it all. And this could not be the case if its dependency or relativity were endless, if all things were dependent for their being upon other things outside themselves, and these in their turn upon others in literally limitless extent. Such a world would not be a cosmos, but a chaos,

'ruining along the illimitable inane.'

The very thought, therefore, of the world's dependence involves, as its correlative, the thought of an independent being undetermined from without.

There is no question of the inevitableness of this conclusion; we cannot avoid it, we cannot unthink it. In Kant's phrase, it regulates all our thought. The only question is whether it merely regulates us as a boundary where thought is baffled, or whether it stands for something that we can in a measure conceive, or, in other words, for a positive idea. Can we positively think of an independent being, which shall sustain all finite and dependent things, without thereby becoming dependent upon them and so losing its identity? Here again personality, and that alone, assists us. As persons we are identical in the midst of change, and on account of our identity we are potentially infinite; for we can progressively appropriate the things and influences outside us, and so transform them, from being limits, into manifestations of ourselves. Thus we are surrounded by other persons, who interfere with and impede our actions; but can win them by affection to become friends, who shall transmit and multiply our own activity. We are imprisoned by foreign languages; but can acquire and thereby transform them from obstacles into instruments of wider access to our kind. We are restrained by laws; but through obedience can make them the means of our development, by making their principles our own. We can even guide the elemental forces, like heat and electricity, from opposing to subserve our will. And in each of these cases the process is the same. We enter spiritually into the alien forms of being that surround us, without losing our identity the while; and so, instead of melting away into modes of them, we make them additional modes of us. While we can even go further in the same direction, by freely creating external objects—statues, pictures, books, machines—for the sole purpose of giving expression and extension to the inner content of ourselves, our feelings and thoughts and wills. Thus though, as finite beings, we too are limited by the outer world, as persons, we can gradually make that world into our own; abolish, as it were, its externality, and make it internal to ourselves; a world within us instead of without us, in which we are no longer slaves, but free. And while we thus reduce alien things into dependence upon our personality, our own independence is not alienated, but intensified by the fact; since, as the things whereon we depend become internal to ourselves, we are increasingly self-dependent. Following this analogy, then, we can conceive of an Infinite Being as One whose only limit is Himself, and who is, therefore, self-determined, self-dependent, self-identical; including the finite, not as a necessary mode, but as a free manifestation of Himself, and thus, while constituting its reality, unaffected by its change—in other words, as an Infinite Person.

The cosmological argument, therefore, is the argument derived from the belief that we recognize in the universe without us certain qualities of infinitude, reality, causation, independence, and the like, which have no counterpart except in the region of our own personality, and can only, therefore, be interpreted as attributes of a person. It does not profess to be a demonstration, and would, of course, involve a fallacy if cast into syllogistic form—the fallacy of drawing a conclusion wider than the premisses. It is rather the intellectual justification of an instinctive intuition, which, as Lotze says, 'has its origin in the very nature of our being.' It is the analysis of the deep conviction which prompts and has prompted man, from immemorial ages, to appeal from the storms of earth to One who sitteth above the water-floods; from the slavery and transiency of earth to One who remaineth a King for ever.

'Change and decay in all around I see:
O Thou who changest not, abide with me.'

And this leads us to the teleological argument[1], or argument from evidences of design in the world. 'Do you not think,' asks Socrates, 'that man's Maker must have given him eyes on purpose that he might see?' with the suggested inference that the existence of eyes must be proof of a purposeful Creator. This argument, from the date of its first

[1] See note 17.

appearance in Greek philosophy, has been one of the strongest supports of natural theology in the ordinary mind. It has had a long controversial history; but none of the objections raised against it have really differed from those which Aristotle saw and answered in his day. 'E pur se muove.' It still retains a weight and impressiveness which show that there is more in it than logical analysis can either detect or refute. The modern doctrine of natural selection, however, has led to the reopening of the question once again. Nature is full of instances of adaptation, and especially adaptation to the future, too numerous, intricate, and various to be the result of chance, and therefore implies a mind. That has been the time-honoured form of the argument; and, consequently, the doctrine of natural selection has been thought to discredit it, by showing that adaptation may, after all, be due to chance. For if a hundred varying organisms came by chance into existence, and ninety-nine of them, being ill-adapted to their surrounding circumstances, perish and are forgotten, the single one which is better adapted to its environment, and therefore survives, will appear to owe to purposeful design what is really due to accidental variation. And if we could conceive this process of natural selection, by survival of the fittest, to have operated exclusively throughout the universe, the result would be an appearance of design without its reality, and the argument from final causes would vanish. Now, natural selection is, of course, a *vera causa*, a principle which undoubtedly obtains throughout the organic world, and the discovery of which has revolutionized our science. But of itself it does not touch the philosophical question of final causes. It has been borrowed for that purpose by materialism, and there is no necessary connexion whatever between its scientific use as an exhibition of nature's method, and its materialistic misuse as a disproof of nature's mind. To begin with, there are many difficulties in the way of our recognizing natural selection as the sole cause of even organic development; while the possibility of its ever accounting for the mechanical and chemical properties of inorganic matter, that already 'manufactured' material, as it has been called, out of which organisms are developed, is, to say the least, extremely doubtful. And, even if all this ground should be one day occupied by natural selection, the original variability of matter, not to mention matter itself, would still remain to be explained. Natural selection acts by selecting variations, and the variations must exist before they can be selected. They cannot of themselves be due to the operation of a principle, of which they are the necessary presupposition. Now, when we speak of chance variations we do not, of course, mean uncaused variations, but merely variations of whose cause—that is, of whose antecedent conditions—we are ignorant. As a matter of fact, the variations of to-day have issued by necessity from those of yesterday, and those of yesterday again from others, carrying us eventually back to the original variability of matter. The present state of the world, therefore, is a necessary consequence of that variability; and, if the present state of the world is full of adaptations which suggest design, the primitive variability from which those adaptations have ensued must suggest it in no less degree. But the materialist conceals this conclusion by shuffling with the word chance, and speaking of 'chance' variations as if they were really accidental. In fact, all variations are rigorously determined; and, if the brains of Plato or St. Paul were results of natural selection, they must none the less have been potentially present in the first condition of the material world. Chance, in the sense of accident, can only have operated before the present system began to be; for there is no room for it inside that system, or it would not be a system. In which case, as Professor Mozley remarks, 'it must have acted up to a certain time, and then issued in its own opposite'; or, in other words, ceased to act. But this is only a popular and pictorial way of saying that chance is unthinkable. Our causal instinct excludes it. And with the exclusion of chance the illegitimate use of natural selection vanishes. For when once we realize that adaptation implies adaptability, and that definite adaptations involve definite determinations of that adaptability, or, in other words, that natural selection can only act upon prepared material, the evidence of design resumes its sway. Materialism in all ages has borrowed its instruments from the physical science of the day; and the present is only one of many similar attempts which have failed in like manner —not from the unsoundness of the scientific instrument, but from the untenable nature of the materialistic position.

Meanwhile, the argument from design has rather gained than lost through modern science. For in its older form it was wont to compare nature, and the various things in nature, to machines or works of art—that is, to objects created for a special purpose, and whose constituent parts are meaningless except in their relation to the whole. This involved an undue separation between nature's means and ends, and often led to strained and artificial conclusions, such as that fruits were designed to feed bird or insect life, when in so doing their more obvious function was destroyed. It was this form of the doctrine that Bacon and Spinoza especially attacked. But we have now come to regard nature as an organic unity, an organism, composed of organisms, and therefore essentially alive. Now it is the characteristic of life, that its every phase and moment is, in a sense, complete in itself, and may be regarded as an end, however much it may conduce to further, fuller, fairer ends to come. Consequently, the absoluteness of the old distinction between means and ends has disappeared. All nature's 'means' are, relatively speaking, ends, and as such have a value of their own. The leaf, and the flower, and the fruit, and the animal's joy in existence, are at the same time ends in themselves, and yet minister to other ends. On the other hand, all nature's ends are, relatively speaking, means. The human eye, for example, considered as an instrument of vision, may be called one of nature's ends—the point where a long line of complex evolution finds its limit; since the very optical defects, with which it has been rashly charged, are now admitted to improve its actual utility. But the eye not only sees, it shines and it speaks—and thus in turn becomes a means of emotional attraction and spiritual intercourse, fairer than the sapphire, more expressive than the tongue; while neither of these qualities can by any possibility be connected with its physical evolution as an instrument of sight. Now a system whose every phase and part, while existing for its own sake, exists also for the sake of the whole, is, if possible, more suggestive of rational design than even a machine would be, especially when it is a progressive system which culminates in the production of a rational being. And thus we may fairly say that modern science, while correcting, has enriched and emphasized the evidence for design. That evidence may not amount to demonstration; and, indeed, logically considered, it is only a section of an argument, for it looks back, for its major premiss, to the previous argument for a first cause, and forward, for its strongest confirmation, to the moral argument, which exhibits the material world as subservient to moral purposes in man. But, taken by itself, the mere spectacle of nature creates an impression upon the imagination which it is difficult to resist. We can often trace purpose in a human creation—a picture or machine—without adequately comprehending what that purpose is. And so with nature. We are conscious of living in the presence of innumerable, exquisite, admirable adaptations, too complex to disentangle, too curious and beautiful to disregard, too infinitely various for any single mind to grasp; which irresistibly suggest the presence of a directing, informing, indwelling reason, that obviously transcends and yet incessantly appeals to our own. And the nearest human analogue for this is to be found, not in the isolated act of reason which creates a work of art, or performs a definite piece of work once for all, but in the continuous consciousness which co-ordinates all the functions of our being, manifesting itself in every momentary thought or word or deed, and thus investing each passing hour with a value of its own, while still controlling and subordinating all, as means, to the attainment of its ultimate end. In other words, we see in nature, not merely an artist or designer, but a person.

Now both the above arguments rest upon the underlying assumption that thought itself is valid, and not a mere chimerical dream; a position which the ordinary Western mind, at least, is perfectly ready to take for granted, but which carries with it an important consequence that is neither so easily accepted nor understood. To think is to know, and the desire for knowledge, which prompts me to think, is part of the very constitution of my mind. But such a desire presupposes a conviction, on my part, that there is something capable of being known—that is, something intelligible. If I come across a children's alphabet, piled up on a table, I do not expect to gain any knowledge from it, because the letters are not arranged; they spell nothing, and are, therefore, unintelligible. But, if I find a book lying open, I at once expect to learn something from it, because its letters are intelligibly arranged and convey a meaning. Now this is the same kind of expectation which underlies all our desire to know the outer world—a conviction that it is intelligible, and therefore can be known. And as we put our desire into operation we find this conviction justified. We find the universe to be a system of mathematical, mechanical, organic, vital, moral relations, which are intelligible and not chaotic. Its letters are arranged. But intelligible relations can only exist through thought, and as the relations in question are certainly independent of all individual human thinkers, they must exist through an universal thought; of which we may say that the individual thinker enters into it, or it into the individual thinker, as we might say in reading a book that we enter into the spirit of the author, or the spirit of the author into us. And as we cannot conceive thought without a thinker, universal thought must mean an absolute or universal mind. Our constitution, as thinking beings, therefore, necessitates our assuming that our thought will correspond with things; which can only be the case if things are intelligible; which, again, can only be the case if they proceed from a mind—and a mind which must be the source of everything that is intelligible, (including all our ideals,) and therefore be the highest which we can think, and therefore, at least, be personal. This initial conviction is, in fact, the beginning of our contact with such a mind, or the beginning of its self-revelation to us, a contact and revelation which increase, as we proceed forward on the path of knowledge. This is the line of thought which is commonly called the ontological proof [1], and which, though often associated exclusively with the names of Anselm and of Descartes, underlies the Platonic ideology, and is developed by Augustine. 'The true meaning of the ontological proof is this,' says Dr. J. Caird—'that as spiritual beings our whole conscious life is based on a universal self-consciousness, an absolute spiritual life, which is not a mere subjective notion or conception, but which carries with it the proof of its necessary existence or reality [2].'

Such, in outline, are the intellectual proofs of the existence of God; suggestions of a probability, which to many minds seem all the more weighty, for their inability to be expressed in syllogistic form. And as the severest criticism of them is associated with the name of Kant (though it has been much qualified by his successors), it is important to remember the object which Kant had in view. It is quite untrue to say that he was inconsistent in his two critiques of the Pure and Practical Reason, feebly attempting to reconstruct in the one what he had successfully destroyed in the other. He definitely regarded the twofold work as one whole, whose final issue was to vindicate the reality of freedom, and through it of God and Immortality. And this work he sought to

---

[1] See note 18. [2] J. Caird, *Philos. of Religion*, p. 159.

accomplish, by first showing that our speculative reason could not act beyond the limits of sensible experience, and could not, therefore, ever either prove or disprove the existence of a God; and then by going on to show that our practical reason, moving in a region beyond phenomenal experience, and consequently beyond the reach of criticism from that region, contains in itself the consciousness of freedom and a moral law; whose realization in the world is the strongest and sufficient evidence of the reality of God, a thing which he never 'for a moment denied or even only doubted.' And whatever view, therefore, we may take of Kant's philosophy, we must not allow the authority of his name to be claimed in favour of an ultimate agnosticism.

This naturally leads us to the crowning argument for the existence of God, and that is the moral argument[1]. It may be stated in a sentence, but cannot be exhausted in a lifetime. It consists in the fact that we are conscious of being free, and yet under the obligation of a moral law, which can only be conceived of as emanating from a personal author.

This is an argument which comes too intimately home to us to need much explanation. 'Our great internal teacher of religion,' says Dr. Newman, 'is our conscience.' 'Conscience is a personal

[1] See note 19.

guide, and I use it because I must use myself. . . . Conscience is nearer to me than any other means of knowledge. . . . Conscience too teaches us not only that God is, but what He is[1].' It is this practical familiarity that we all have with conscience which makes the appeal of the moral argument so strong. But clouds of controversy have gathered round it and confused its outline: battle has been joined upon irrelevant issues; and the ill-advised retention of obsolete forms of defence has often given its opponents an apparent advantage. There may be some use, therefore, in a brief statement of the case. The argument in question starts from two facts of consciousness—freedom and obligation. We have already referred to the fact that freedom is rooted in our self-consciousness, but it will be well to return for a moment to this point. I find myself in a world whose events and phases are causally connected in one indissoluble chain, and my bodily organism is an inseparable part of that world. I do not, therefore, profess to be capriciously independent of what is called the universal reign of law. But I possess this peculiarity—that, whereas all other things in the world are necessarily determined by external agencies or causes, I have the power to make the external influences which affect my conduct my own, before allowing them to do so, thereby converting them from alien forces

[1] *Grammar of Assent.*

into inner laws; so that when determined by them I am not determined from without but from within. This process is best exhibited in the case of bodily appetites and desires; because they so obviously connect us with the material world and its inevitable order, that there, if anywhere, I shall find myself a slave. What, then, is the process of acting from such a desire? We feel a desire and act accordingly. But something intervenes between our feeling the desire and initiating the act. The desire does not draw the action after it as one physical event draws on another. We must first say to ourselves, however implicitly and half-unconsciously, 'The satisfaction of this desire will gratify me, and therefore I will satisfy it.' In other words, I represent the satisfaction of the desire, in imagination, as an ideal or end or object to myself. I represent myself satisfied to myself desiring, I picture myself to myself, myself as object to myself as subject. And it is not the physical effect of the desire, the mere pathological feeling, but the metaphysical action of the mental image that ultimately determines my action or is my motive. Now it is impossible to maintain that during this process the mind is only a passive spectator of what is going on within it. It consciously takes up the raw material of desire into its own spiritual machinery, and there manufactures it into motives. And this it can only do through its self-consciousness, or power of turning round upon itself, and looking itself in the face, thus distinguishing itself into subject and object; since this enables it to transform its various subjective feelings and affections into objects; transferring them, as it were, with a change of sign, from the subjective to the objective side of the equation, where, as being objects, they can be discussed, compared, rejected or pursued. In other words, we must cut our physical feelings out of their physical context before we act upon them, and cannot, therefore, be governed by the necessity attaching to them; since they only retain this necessity while continuing in their context as part of the material world. The truth of this analysis will obviously not be affected by the nature of the feeling in question. It applies equally to all the materials out of which motives can be made—bodily appetite, altruistic sympathies and sentiments, and the sanctions of positive law. For the rewards and penalties of positive law can no more constrain us than our physical desires. They cannot begin to act till there is a self-consciousness which can present them as objects to itself, and thus translate them into motives, however incapable the savage mind may be of analyzing such a process. In the very fact of saying 'This is the law' I separate myself from it; I put it outside myself; I stand aloof from it, and thereby break the inevitable necessity with which it may appear at first sight to enchain me. If I then proceed to reunite myself with it by obedience, or make it my motive, I do so of my own accord. I act, as Kant says, not from the law, but from the consciousness of the law. However strongly, therefore, positive law may urge me to act, I must appropriate it and make it *my* law before it can do so. It is in this capacity for creating, or co-operating in the creation of my own motives, with the selective power which it inevitably implies, that my freedom consists—being, in fact, a conditioned or constitutional freedom. It rests on the guarantee of my own self-consciousness, of which, in truth, it is a necessary property; and in the nature of the case it can never be criticized or explained by any science; for science can only deal with objects; and freedom can never become an object, being an inalienable function of my subjectivity or self.

Freedom, then, is a point upon which we can allow no shuffling or juggling in argument. It is unique, but it is self-evident; and every attempt to explain it away can be shown to involve a *petitio principii* or begging of the question.

It is otherwise with our next point—the sense of duty or moral obligation; for this has a history behind it, whose early stages are obscure and consequently leave room for conjecture. Still it will simplify this history to bear carefully in mind the distinction between the form and the matter or contents of the moral law. The latter—that is to say the sum total of particular duties which constitute the morality of a nation or a man—varies, and has always varied, in different places and times. But the very fact of these variations only throws into stronger relief the constancy of the formal element, or sense of obligation, which is common to them all. For if a thousand people think themselves to have a thousand different duties, their divergence in detail does but emphasize the general sense of duty wherein they agree.

Turning then to history, with this distinction in mind, we find the sense of duty or obligation in every civilized race. It has never been more powerfully expressed than by the pre-Christian moralists of Greece and Rome, and modern research has found it clearly recognized in the most remote antiquity—of India, Persia, and China, of Babylon and Egypt. Men may not have acted up to it any more than they do now; still there it always was, explicitly accepted by the higher minds, and capable of being addressed as implicitly present in the lower. But it is suggested that the case is different in what may be called hypothetical history—that is, the history of primitive man as reconstructed on the analogy of the modern savage. The fact that the modern savage is still a savage might fairly be urged as a considerable qualification of his claim to represent primitive man, who, *ex hypothesi*, must have been the parent of all the progressive peoples. His condition is far more suggestive of degradation than of primitive integrity. Nor, even if this point be waived, is there any sufficient evidence that uncivilized races are unmoral. Their morality is not indeed the morality of civilization—that is to say, its content is different from ours. But it by no means follows, as is often far too readily assumed, that they have no latent moral faculty or sense of obligation. On the contrary, there is a world-wide institution which points in the opposite direction—namely, the system of taboo. Taboo includes the twofold notion of religious reverence and religious abhorrence—awe of trespassing upon certain places, and things, and persons that are sacred, and fear of contact with certain others which are profane. Now, if we separate the content of this law of taboo—that is to say, the details which it prescribes or proscribes—from the sanctions on which it rests, we find the latter to be closely analogous to, if not identical with, the moral sanctions of civilization; either religious hope and fear, or an unaccountable sense of obligation, so strong that its violation sometimes issues in death. And, in face of this fact, it may be fairly asserted, that uncivilized races give no support to the theory of an unmoral condition of humanity. Quatrefages goes so far as to say that 'the fundamental identity of human nature is nowhere more strikingly displayed' than in the moral region [1].

There is really no necessity, however, in defending our argument, to follow its opponents into this obscure region. The verdict of authentic history is enough. For 'things are what they are' quite irrespectively of how they came to be. The truth of astronomical discoveries is not affected by the fact, that the faculty which makes them could not formerly count four. Neither is the inference from the moral sense to be discredited, because the process of its evolution has been gradual.

The inference is this: man is conscious of an imperative obligation upon his conduct. It is not a physical necessity, disguised in any shape or form, for he is also conscious of being free either to accept or to decline it. It cannot originate within him, for he has no power to unmake it; and it accomplishes purposes which its agent does not at the time foresee—results to himself and others which he can recognize afterwards as rational, but which his own individual reason could never have designed. It cannot be the voice of other men, though human law may give it partial utterance; for it speaks to his motives, which no law can fathom, and calls him to attainments which no law can reach. Yet, with all its indepen-

[1] *Human Species.*

dence of human authorship, it has the notes of personality about it. It commands our will with an authority which we can only attribute to a conscious will. It constrains us to modes of action which are not of our own seeking, yet which issue in results that only reason could have planned. It educates our character with a nicety of influence irresistibly suggestive of paternal care. The philosophers who have probed it, the saints and heroes who have obeyed and loved it, the sinners who have defied it, are agreed in this. And the inevitable inference must be that it is the voice of a Personal God.

Such is the moral argument in outline; and it must be viewed as a whole to feel its force. The authority of the moral law must not be severed from its rationality, for it is in their combination that its evidential significance consists. It commands us, and we obey it blindly, as regards any distinct foresight of its results; yet this blind obedience invariably issues in such personal development and social progress as imply providential design. And it is this teleological character of moral obligation that makes the mode of its first appearance unimportant. Freedom, its presupposition, we must and can successfully defend. But we are bound to no particular theory of the historic emergence of the moral sense. For its evolution is its vindication; what it is proves what it was. The spiritual results which it has realized show the spiritual nature of its cause.

This argument obviously corroborates those which have gone before, for it resumes them all upon a higher plane. It increases our necessity for believing in a free first cause; it shows the reason in the world to be, moreover, a righteous reason; and it intensifies the evidence of design. It thus crowns the convergence of probable arguments which spring from the very centre of our personal consciousness, and can only be even plausibly refuted on the assumption that that consciousness itself is fundamentally untrue.

LECTURE V

MORAL AFFINITY NEEDFUL FOR THE KNOWLEDGE OF A PERSON

IF the arguments in favour of belief in the personality of God are as numerous and as weighty as we have seen them to be, the question naturally arises, How can speculative agnosticism seem so plausible, and practical agnosticism be so common as it is? Self-communication is of the essence of personality. If, therefore, God be personal, why is He not universally known, why has He not more conspicuously revealed Himself, as such? To answer this question we must examine both past religious history and present religious experience. But we must begin with the present (πρότερον ἡμῖν); for otherwise we have no clue to the phenomena of the past, no thread upon which to string its facts; and the attempt to interpret religious history, without previous insight into religious experience, is a fruitful source of error.

What, then, do we mean by the knowledge of a Personal God? What do we expect it to be like? How do religious men describe it?

To begin with, all knowledge is a process, or the result of a process, conscious or implicit. The simplest knowledge is founded upon sensitive perception, and the ordinary man imagines that sensitive perception is involuntary; he cannot help hearing or seeing or feeling a thing if it is there. But a very little psychology will undeceive him. Not only do we read mental categories or forms into the reports of sensation, before they can become 'things' at all, but sensation itself involves attention, which is an act of will, and will is always determined by more or less desire; so that even in sensitive perception there is an active exercise of all the three functions of our personality—thought, emotion, and will. The process, indeed, in common cases, has become so automatic as to appear involuntary; but if we watch children beginning to take notice of things, or if we set ourselves to observe any new class of phenomena, for a scientific or artistic purpose, we at once discover the activity, and the threefold nature of the activity required. The sensible world is there; but our whole personality must co-operate in the knowing of it.

The same thing happens on a larger scale in the case of scientific knowledge. The unscientific man and the sciolist are apt to think that it is purely intellectual, and comes naturally to a certain class of mind. But if we look at the world's real thinkers, and the lives that they have led, we see at once, that emotional and moral qualities, of no mean order, are involved in the successful pursuit of even the simplest science; while the two men who are most associated, in the English mind, with the development of scientific method—F. Bacon and J. S. Mill—are equally emphatic in tracing intellectual fallacies to ethical causes, in other words, to the emotions and the will. If we take a physical science, for example, we see at once what a call it makes both on the character and conduct of the student who would succeed in its pursuit. There must be a degree of detachment, which may fairly be called ascetic, from intellectual as well as social distractions; freedom from the mental indolence that allows men to acquiesce in premature conclusions, as well as from all prejudice, whether of habit or inclination; infinite patience; unflagging perseverance; and the enthusiasm which alone makes patience and perseverance possible. Here again, then, though the subject-matter exists outside the man, an active co-operation of all his faculties is needful for its knowledge.

Again, if we turn from abstract to human interests, from natural to social science, the same law is even more conspicuous. For the political or social philosopher must be at least as patient, as persevering, as independent, as enthusiastic as the biologist or chemist. But social science is essentially practical. Practical utility is the object for which it is acquired, as well as its only experimental test. Its possessor, therefore, must naturally carry it into practice, and this will involve sympathy and courage; for he is not confronted, like the physical experimentalist, by inanimate matter, but by human beings with hearts and passions that react upon his own. If he quails before their antagonism, or is misled by respect of persons, and stands aside, as Plato sadly says, 'unhelpful from the storm behind the wall,' his theories will remain untested, unverified, unreal, the dreams of a doctrinaire. But if he determines to realize his knowledge, whether as a statesman or reformer or philanthropist, he must leave the study for the market-place, and face the fate of patriots—misunderstanding, misrepresentation, disappointment, probable danger, possible death. Thus the fact, that the subject-matter of the social sciences is personal, intensifies their reaction upon the entire personality of their student.

Now we go through a similar process in acquiring the real knowledge of a person. This may not be at first sight obvious, because men so seldom attempt to know the inner nature of the people who surround them. They are content to know them in what may be called an abstract way—in one or more of their various aspects, their business capacities, or social habits, or scientific attainments, or political opinions, or poetical ideas. And it is only once and again under pressure of reverence or love that we crave to pass through these partial manifestations to the character behind them. And then, in proportion to the depth and greatness of the character in question, is the difficulty of really coming to know it. We may easily idolize, or underestimate a man, but to know him as he is—his true motives, the secret springs of his conduct, the measure of his abilities, the explanation of his inconsistencies, the nature of his esoteric feelings, the dominant principle of his inner life—this is often a work of years, and one in which our own character, and conduct, play quite as important a part as our understanding : for not only must the necessary insight be the result of our own acquired capacities—which will have to be great, in proportion to the greatness of the personality with which we have to deal—but there must further exist the kind and degree of affinity between us, which can alone make self-revelation on his part possible. Plato, for instance, the spiritual philosopher, saw more profoundly into Socrates, than could Xenophon, his companion in arms. Shakespeare and de Balzac, in their different spheres, were unrivalled students of humanity : yet the latter could not see in it pure womanhood; the former has never painted a saint; so essentially is even the intuition of genius qualified by character.

We find then, upon analysis, that an element of will, and emotion, is obscurely present in even the simplest beginnings of knowledge. As we pass from ordinary to scientific thinking, the action of this moral factor is intensified; while it becomes more prominent still in those branches of study whose object is humanity, and therefore whose proper perfection involves their practice; and, finally, in the process of acquiring the knowledge of a person, assumes an entirely preponderant importance.

Now, if we believe in a Personal God, we must believe that our knowledge of Him will be analogous in method to our knowledge of human personality. The various aspects of nature, with which the different sciences deal, must indeed be conceived of as thoughts of the divine mind, divine ideas, and to that extent manifestations of the divine character; but taken by themselves they will no more adequately reveal the personality of their Author than do the external habits, the isolated acts, the occasional speeches of a man. They may arrest our attention by their pregnant suggestiveness, and lead us to look beyond them, but by themselves they convey no knowledge of what is beyond. All that the mathematician knows is that the universe is mathematically arranged; while the biologist sees, further, in it an immanent teleology, and the artist forms of beauty. But, however much these things may suggest a personality behind them, they do not, and it is obvious, by the nature of the case, that they cannot, afford any knowledge upon the subject. As branches of knowledge, in the strict sense of the term, they begin and end with themselves; and the man who claimed to have swept the heavens with his telescope, and seen no God, was doubtless astronomically accurate. When, indeed, we pass from the natural to the moral sciences, we come near to the evidence for a Personal God; but it is only a kind of circumstantial evidence. Our inner recognition of a moral law, and our external observation of its inexorable justice, its severe beneficence, its ultimate triumph, are, as we have already seen, among the strongest arguments of natural religion. But still they are only arguments; they point to a Person, but they are not that Person. Law is universal in its action; it does not individualize; it has no equity, no mercy; it does not behave like a person. And accordingly the history of speculation exhibits many schools of thought which, while fully recognizing the moral law both in their theory and their practice, have yet never regarded it otherwise than as an impersonal power making for righteousness. Moral philosophy, therefore, and even moral conduct, however near to Him they may lead us, will not of themselves give us the knowledge of a Personal God. There is still something abstract and general about them; whereas the knowledge of a person is essentially individual and concrete.

Clearly, then, if we would know God as personal, we must specialize our study with that view: we must begin with a desire to know Himself, as distinct from His manifestations in nature, or His works in the world. And it is obvious that, in proportion to the awfulness of His personality, this desire must be both intense and sincere. We have already seen the impossibility of trifling with a natural, or moral science, or a human friendship, and the seriousness with which they must be approached; and it will hardly be denied, that to trifle with the study of the Infinite Source of all these things, must be yet more impossible still. This desire, therefore, must be sincere, in the sense that it has no critical or experimental aim, such as the justification of a theory or the refutation of an opponent; and it must be intense enough to counterbalance the multitude of desires which conflict with it, and enable its possessor, in his measure, to make the words of the Psalmist his own: 'There is none upon earth that I desire in comparison of Thee.'

Further, moral affinity is an essential of personal intimacy. A man cannot understand a character with which his own has no accord. And affinity with a Holy Being implies a progressive and lifelong effort of the will. The moral virtues which we have seen to be necessary for success in science are departmental, and do not cover the whole range of conduct: some are needed, and others not. But to know a Person, who is perfectly holy, we must focus our entire moral character upon Him, for such holiness partakes of the unity of the Person in whom it dwells, and, however various its manifestations, is yet absolutely one. Now such an effort of the will is not easy either of attainment or of maintenance; and still it is not all. We have a past, and an inheritance of sin and infirmity upon us, which the secular moralist counsels us to obliterate, by the simple process of amendment. But amendment is not enough, or rather it is not a simple process, if we view sin as not only the breach of a law, but as also disobedience to a Person whom we now desire to know. 'Against Thee only have I sinned and done this evil in Thy sight' has been the cry of religion the whole world over; and, so far from its bitterness being diminished as religious views grow more refined, it is more acutely terrible to realize that we have wronged our Father, or our Lover, than our Master, or our Judge. Penitence of heart, therefore, or contrition would seem a necessary element in the purification of those who would know God. And as this is a point on which religion is often vehemently attacked, in the name and supposed interests of the higher morality, we may recur for its justification to human analogy. Who that has ever wronged a parent, a benefactor, a lover, or a friend, does not know, as a matter of experience, not only the naturalness of emotional as distinct from 'ethical repentance'—of sorrow, that is to say, as distinct from mere amendment—but also its necessity, before mutual understanding can be restored, and the increase of that necessity, in proportion to the degree of the love wounded, and the wrong done? This is not a matter of external propriety, but a psychological law which there is no evading: without emotional repentance we must part, or remain on a lower level of intercourse, but we cannot grow in intimacy, and the insight which intimacy brings. And the question with which we are now dealing, it must be remembered, is precisely this—not moral character by itself, but moral character considered as a qualification for the personal knowledge of a Personal God. Human analogy, therefore, is in our favour when we maintain that this character must be penitent as well as progressive, sorrowful of heart as well as resolute of will.

Finally, it is obvious that these moral and emotional conditions will not only accompany but influence the proper action of the intellect; inducing earnestness, energy, patience with adverse appearances, susceptibility to slight impressions, quickness to catch hints, appreciativeness, moderation, humility, delicacy, fineness. The pain and sorrow of life, for instance, which, abstractedly considered, are a perplexity, gradually cease to be so, to the man who is sincere enough to recognize their punitive and purifying effects in his own history. The uniform laws, which from without look so mechanical, are surprisingly adapted to his individual condition when honestly viewed from within. The obscurity of revelation, or the uncertainty of conscience, are no greater than he feels his due, after trifling with them so often in the past. In this way intellectual difficulties, one after another, fade away, or at least sink into subordinate importance, before a mind that has been duly qualified by moral discipline for their investigation; while, on the other hand, evidences and arguments, which in formal statement are only probable, assume, for the individual, a colour and complexion which ultimately raise them almost to the certainty of an intuition. And this clarification, and control of the intellectual by the moral faculties, is in complete harmony with the analogy which we have been following throughout. For the simplest-minded friend or servant knows far more of a man's true character, than a stranger or an enemy however intellectually able.

So far we have been considering the knowledge of God from its purely human side; but the cogency of our conclusion is still further emphasized when we turn to the other aspect of the question, and ask under what conditions His revelation of Himself as personal would, on the same analogy, be naturally made. The same limitations, which qualify our power of knowing a person, qualify also the possibility of his making himself known to us. We have already seen how this is the case in our human relations, and we should expect it to be still more true of a divine revelation. For a Person who is holy cannot reveal Himself as such to the unholy, since they do not know holiness when they see it; and it appears to them unintelligible, terrible, even hateful; anything, in short, but what it really is. A Person who is loving, in the true sense of the word, cannot reveal Himself as such to those who have no notion that love must involve sacrifice, and has in it, therefore, an awful element of sternness; for to them love would not appear love, but its opposite. An Infinite Person cannot reveal Himself as such to one who, unconscious of his own limitations, persists in measuring all things by the standard of a finite capacity, and denying the existence of what he cannot comprehend. And again, even where there is both desire and aptitude for the revelation, a Person can only reveal Himself partially and gradually, in proportion as these qualifications progressively increase; and we must remember what searchings of heart, and agony of will, that increase, as we have seen, must of necessity imply. And if it be objected to all this, that we cannot imagine, *a priori*, what the conditions of a divine communication are likely to be, it is sufficient answer that belief in a Personal God means nothing else, than belief in One who acts towards us as persons act, and therefore to whose action human analogies may be applied.

Briefly to resume, then: if God is personal, analogy would lead us to suppose that He must be known as a person is known—that is, first, by a special study distinct from any other, and secondly, by an active exercise of our whole personality, in which the will, the faculty through which alone our personality acts as a whole, must of necessity predominate; while in proportion to His transcendent greatness, will be the seriousness of the call, which the knowledge of Him makes upon our energies.

Now, it will hardly be denied that in much modern discussion of religious belief these momentous requirements are overlooked; with the result that negative opinions are prematurely adopted, as the result not of profound but of undisciplined investigation. It is continually taken for granted that scientific or critical attainments, or even their intelligent appreciation at second-hand, qualify a man for discussing the personality of God, as if it were a corollary, positive or negative, from one or more of the special sciences, and not, so to say, a science *sui generis*, with prerequisites and methods of its own. And it naturally follows that the doctrine in question is viewed as purely intellectual, and the ascription of its disbelief to moral causes resented as an impertinence. Nor can the blame of this mistake be said to lie wholly on one side. Controversy may sometimes become too courteous, and, in its righteous reaction against bygone intolerance, forget that toleration has its weak side also. And the fear of seeming to impute motives to individual opponents, or the anxiety to do full justice to an adverse point of view, often leads to a degree of apologetic understatement, which conceals essential differences beneath a surface of agreement, and is in fact, therefore, though not in intention, insincere. The principle that character and conduct are the keys to creed, and that we are, therefore, more responsible for our intellectual behaviour than is often supposed, is precisely one of those points which, amid the civilities of polite debate, is apt to be insufficiently maintained. All analogy, however, is, as we have seen, unmistakably in its favour, and a very moderate amount of introspection should suffice to convince us of its truth.

Of course the blinding influence of such things as indolence, or sensuality, or vanity, or pride, or avarice, or deliberate selfishness in any form, is too plainly obvious to be denied. But what is denied, as we have already seen, is that a measure of this blinding influence may continue, long after its causes have been practically overcome; and consequently that a penitential process, more profound even than moral amendment, is in all such cases necessary for the restoration of the spiritual vision. And yet this is not only the universal teaching of the Christian Church in every age, but of many a pre-Christian and extra-Christian thinker; and it cannot fail to be justified by sincere self-examination. It is no burden complacently imposed upon the human spirit by men who had not felt its weight. It has been taught, because it has been experienced, and its teachers have only required of others the same discipline, which they themselves have with much suffering gone through. 'He must become godlike,' says Plotinus, 'who desires to see God.'

Again, there are less obviously immoral tendencies —such as intellectual ambition, the need of controversial consistency, the subtle desire to increase or retain an influence, the speculative irreverence of youth, the desponding tone of age—which easily escape our notice, yet, unless detected and subdued, will distort and deflect the action of our judgement from its true course in examining the things of the spirit.

And again, there are still slighter defects, which often pass as intellectual, and yet which on reflection can be seen to be of moral origin, and, like the infinitesimal aberration of an astronomical instrument, vitiate our entire observation. For example, the above-mentioned assumption, that the knowledge of God is primarily intellectual, involves, on the face of it, an undervaluing of His attribute of holiness. The assertion that our faculties cannot apprehend what they cannot comprehend, cannot feel what they do not understand, implies a more complete self-knowledge than we in fact possess. The kindred denial, that spiritual experience may be as real as physical experience, casts a slur upon the mental capacity of many of the greatest of our race, from which true humility would shrink. The transference of the method of one science to the pursuit of another, the neglect to distinguish clearly between hypothesis and fact, the undue bias of the imagination by special kinds of study, the premature deduction of negative conclusions—the dangers, in fact, of specialism in an age when knowledge is increasingly specialized—are more often admitted in word than really in practice avoided. And though these and such-like imperfections may seem to many to be trivial, when regarded from a moral point of view, they are not so in the particular context and connexion with which we are now concerned; and still less so in the case of teachers (and every writer is a teacher) who would abolish an august tradition, coeval with recorded history, and involving the highest hopes and aspirations of mankind.

Of course it is not to be contended that these moral dispositions are the exclusive cause of intellectual error in religion. As there are countless professed believers, whose orthodoxy has never touched their hearts, and who may therefore be called spiritually dead, so there are unbelievers whose conduct and emotions are in continual rebellion against the limitations of their creed, and who, for all their unbelief, therefore, are spiritually alive. But, however numerous these cases, they are the exception and not the rule, and do not alter our conviction that average agnosticism is in one or other of the many ways above described of moral origin; while the impossibility, as well as the impropriety, of judging individual opponents, makes it all the more necessary to emphasize the importance of the principle in general. There is no arrogance in so doing: the arrogance, on the contrary, lies with those who expect to attain a specific kind of knowledge without undergoing its appropriate discipline [1]. At the same time, so serious a statement, with the grave charge that

[1] See note 20.

it implies, would never have been put forward, as it has been by Christians in every age, if it rested only upon probable reasoning. The analogy which we have been pursuing *a priori* has been abundantly verified in personal experience, and indeed in many cases represents the analysis rather than the antecedent of that experience. And this inductive verification, as in logical language it may be called, is an essential part of its argumentative presentation. We must turn, therefore, to the Christian or Theistic consciousness, and view the operation, as seen from within, of the process which we have hitherto been discussing from without.

Its point of departure, then, is the point to which analogy has conducted us, the necessity of holiness, and therefore of purification. True, there are the Galahads and Percevals of life—those for whom 'the vision splendid' of all that is lovely and of good report has never lost its fascination or 'faded into the light of common day'—as well as those who have realized a measure of the bitterness of Dante's words:

> 'Tanto giu cadde che tutti argomenti
> Alla salute sua eran gia corti
> Fuor che monstrarli le perdute genti.'

But the clear insight of the innocent, in proportion to its purity, sees altitudes of possible attainment, and detects degrees of contaminating evil, which are alike beyond the range of ordinary eyes; and is only, therefore, the more acutely, sensitively conscious of its own share in the universal human need of purification. But this purification, when, in independence of all inferior sanctions, it is viewed as taking place under the immediate eye of God, assumes at once a new extent and a new intensity. For its standard is then perfection and its consequent inadequacy infinite. Attraction to the beauty of holiness, or aversion from the spectacle of sin, love of God, or hatred of self, may be the dominant passion of the soul; but the result in either case is similar—a sense of hopeless, helpless impotence to attain the one, or to avoid the other. This sense of incapacity is specifically religious. It goes beyond any analogy that can be drawn from human intercourse. Nor can it exist in any ethical system, whose standard is relative, or whose sanctions hypothetical. For a relative standard may be attained with effort, and an hypothetical sanction may be declined at will. But union with God can neither be attained nor yet declined by man; it is felt to be imperative, yet seems to be impossible. And hence issues the universal cry of all true religion— 'Make me a clean heart, O God, and renew a right spirit within me.' That may be done from the divine side which cannot be done from the human. And from the conviction that this cry is answered, comes the assurance that we are in contact with a Personal God. The paths which may lead men to this conviction are various, the circumstances which surround it various, the modes of its description various—differing in different religions, and different individuals; but the essential fact is the same—that the human cry has been divinely answered.

Here, then, we are in the presence of a new fact, which is usually called 'supernatural,' and may most conveniently be called so still, in the sense that it comes from the spiritual region, in contrast with that which in ordinary language we are accustomed to call natural. And a new fact is simply a matter of experience. It may be argued against as impossible, or argued for as probable; but neither argument can really touch it; it either has or has not been experienced, and with that the question ends. What, then, is the evidence of the reality of religious experience? Common sense, and scientific criticism, and medical pathology may freely prune its excentricities to the limit of their will. But there remains an immense and unexplained residuum, of the best and noblest of our race, men and women, who in every age and in every rank and station, and endowed with every degree and kind of intellectual capacity, have lived the lives of saints and heroes, or died the death of martyrs, and furthered by their action and passion, and, as they trusted, by their prayers, the material, moral, social, spiritual welfare of mankind, solely in reliance on their personal intercourse with God. Materialism is obliged to explain their experience away, as a reflex action misinterpreted, or other form of hallucination; with the awkward result of having to attribute the finest types of human character, as well as the greatest factor in the progress of the world, to the direct action of mental disease. But materialism already labours under difficulties enough of its own. All, however, who, on the other hand, admit the probability, or even the possibility of a Personal God, must be arrested by the spectacle of 'this great cloud of witnesses' claiming to have known Him as a person is known. It is a distinct additional argument, and one more easily ignored than answered. The fact attested is an interior certainty of personal intercourse with God, and as such is quite distinct from any consequence or doctrine in whose favour it may be subsequently used; a purely spiritual fact. The persons who attest it are a minority of religious people, and not, therefore, to be confused with those who merely believe in its possibility, without professing its experience; but though a relative minority, they are strictly 'a multitude whom no man can number'—competent, capable, sane, of no one type or temperament, as old as authentic history, as numerous as ever in the world to-day; a far more searchingly sifted and universally extended body of observers than can be quoted in behalf of any single scientific fact. We are fairly entitled, therefore, to claim this accumulated mass of consentient evidence, as a powerful confirmation of all our other arguments.

The process which analogy suggests, then, is the process which the saints have followed, and they assure us that by following it they have reached their goal—the personal knowledge of a Personal God. It is a process which, as we have seen, involves the action of our entire personality, both in its extent and its intensity, its wholeness and its oneness. 'God,' says Plato, 'holds the soul attached to Him by its root'; and it is not till we get down to this root of the soul, the 'I,' that is more fundamental than all its faculties or functions, that we feel the need of that communion with Him, which is in reality an evidence that He is already in communion with us. 'Tetigisti me et exarsi in pacem tuam.' Hence it is a process whose every moment is instinct with life, and which no amount of abstract language can adequately represent. To be realized in its full force, whether of example or of argument, it must be watched in those who are living it, or studied as recorded in the Psalter, the Epistle to the Romans, the Confessions of Augustine, the German Theology, the Imitation of Christ, and the countless lesser spiritual biographies of holy and humble men of heart, who have lived it and departed in its peace.

Now an important consequence which follows from all this is that religious knowledge, in the sense above described—knowledge of God as distinct from opinion about Him—is of the nature of a personal and private property, peculiar to its possessor, and which others cannot share. This is a fact which in controversy is apt to be ignored; and its assertion is sometimes resented. Yet, again, universal analogy is in its favour. Scientific truth, too, is the personal possession of the earnest experimentalist, who for the sake of it has 'scorned delights and lived laborious days'; and in proportion to the degree of his advance in it he is alone. Even when its discoveries, such as steam or electricity or chloroform, are embodied for popular use in practical appliances, we know the danger of such appliances in ignorant, untutored hands; and its speculative results are equally unmeaning and unsafe, in the mouth of the sciolist who knows nothing of the method or discipline of their attainment. So, again, in the intimacy of friends there are secrets shared, and privileges granted, and sacred thoughts exhibited, of which no stranger is allowed a glimpse. The privacy of religious knowledge, therefore, is only the privacy of all knowledge carried to a further degree. The religious man cannot communicate the inner secret of his life. He may be able to lay before inquirers a reason for the faith that is in him, proofs of the existence of God, and of the reasonableness of revelation, and of its preponderant probability over adverse theories: but he feels the while that these arguments cannot of themselves insure conviction, and have in his own case been supplemented from other and more esoteric sources, too secret, too subtle, too spiritual, too sacred to produce. Influences that have been brought to bear on him, events that have been controlled for him, strangely occurrent voices of prophet, or of psalmist, speaking to him suddenly in crises of his life; prayers answered, efforts assisted, purposes thwarted, providence felt; warnings of God in disease and dreams, judgements unmistakable of God on other men; punishments, consolations, moments of spiritual insight; memories of saints; examples of friends —these, and such-like things, as they have gathered round his history, are the ground of his inner certitude that he is living face to face with One who 'knoweth his downsitting and his uprising and understandeth his thoughts long before'; who 'is about his path and about his bed, and spieth out all his ways.' Naturally the subject of such experience as this does not expect others to be convinced by it. It is his experience, and not another's, and is conclusive to him alone. Now and again a great religious teacher lays bare the secrets of his inmost spirit, less for the conviction of opponents than for the confirmation of kindred souls: but most men, who are at all conscious of them, keep these things and ponder them in their hearts; with the result that both their force and frequency are underrated by the external critic, and things attributed to exceptional superstition, or hallucination, that in reality are normal episodes in the spiritual life. For the purposes of our analogy we have been obliged to speak of this spiritual life, as if the knowledge of it only supervened at a certain stage upon the use of our natural faculties. But in reality it is only explicitly known at the end, because it is implicitly contained in the beginning. As reason qualifies and conditions our whole animal nature by its presence, so that we are never merely animals, spirituality also permeates and modifies all that we call our natural faculties; and our personality itself is, in this sense, as truly supernatural as the Divine Person in whom alone it finds its home.

LECTURE VI

RELIGION IN THE PREHISTORIC PERIOD

IT is natural that, in proportion to the strength of our belief in a Personal God, we should expect that He would reveal Himself to man; not merely to a favoured few, but to the human race as such. For the desire of self-communication is, as we have seen, an essential function of our own personality; it is part of what we mean by the word; and we cannot conceive a Person freely creating persons, except with a view to hold intercourse with them when created. So necessary, indeed, is this deduction that, unless it were justified by historic facts, a strong presumption would be created against the truth of the belief from which it flows. Yet there can be no question that, on appealing to history, we do not at first sight find this expectation at all adequately met. Hence the importance of bearing in mind the many serious limitations under which, as we have seen above, any revelation must be made. For men often seem to anticipate too much, and for that very reason to find too little evidence of a divine revelation in history. Our analysis of the nature of personality certainly leads us to expect, that God will reveal Himself as personal to every created person. But all that this expectation can possibly involve is an ultimate revelation. It carries with it no further idea of how or when, of time or method. And inasmuch as our belief in God is intimately bound up with a belief in immortality, we have no shadow of a reason, *a priori*, for limiting His revelation to this world. Life on earth may be to many but an infant-school; and the savage may be called to leave it with no calculable progress made, no visible result attained; and yet with much inner preparation for the stage which is to come, even if it be confined to the bitter negative induction, 'by the means of the evil that good is the best.' If the end of education is fitness for fellowship with God, there is nothing surprising in the slowness of its pace. For the two great obstacles to all improvement of character are indolence and impatience, and a premature degree of revelation would minister to both—by giving men more than their conduct as yet entitled them to ask, or their capacities as yet enabled them to use. We have already seen how many conditions, qualifications, limitations, hindrances modify the spiritual insight of all ordinary minds, even when in the presence of the holiest traditions, and under the influence of the highest moral code. It should be no cause for surprise, therefore, that the signs of such insight grow more rare, as we travel back into the remoter regions of the past. And yet without insight revelation is impossible; for the fruition must presuppose the faculty.

While, then, we naturally anticipate some kind of universal revelation, we have no reason to be disconcerted, on finding that its evidence is less clear, or less abundant than we might have previously supposed. But, on the other hand, we must not for a moment allow the opponents of revelation to beg the question, by interpreting history upon an irreligious hypothesis, and thus neutralizing from the outset all the evidence that may exist. It is not unnatural that the collectors of religious phenomena—the religious archaeologists and antiquarians, the founders and frequenters of museums of comparative religion—should describe the facts which they discover from a purely external or scientific point of view: but we must remember that such description, in proportion as it becomes habitual, indisposes us to recognize a divine counterpart to human creeds; and thus requires a continual correction of its bias. For only the religious can legitimately estimate religion. And the religions of the past can never be rightly understood, except in the light of the religion of the present. Faith and conscience must be known as they now are, before their earlier manifestations can be recognized. We are often, indeed, warned against the fallacy of reading modern ideas into bygone ages; and the warning has its value. But it is equally fallacious to suppose that we can isolate the past, and study it without assistance from the present. For there are no such things as isolated facts. The simplest fact of observation is, as we have already seen, partly created by the observer's mind; and the more complex a fact becomes, the more elaborate is its intellectual setting. Now, the facts of the far past, that have come down to us, are like fragments that have dropped out of their context; and to understand them properly we must reconstruct their context by an imaginative effort, in which analogies drawn from the present are our inevitable guides. In cases which do not admit of controversy this process often goes on unnoticed—as when we find a flint arrow-head, and immediately infer its purpose, and its author's habits. But in controverted questions it sometimes seems to be assumed that we can avoid the operation altogether, whereas all that we can really do is to be accurate and heedful in its performance—discriminating the element of fact from the element of imagination, and taking care that facts shall not be first coloured by a theory, and then employed as evidence of its truth. The real danger lies, not in reading our own presuppositions into history, but in doing so without being aware of it, and without calling attention to the fact, so that due critical precautions may be observed. When, for instance, we find it stated, as the result of a comparison of religions, that all religion is a human invention and therefore equally false, or that all religion is equally inspired and therefore equally true, or that the inspiration of one is emphasized by the conspicuous falsehood of the remainder, such extreme generalizations are obviously due to the unguarded prepossessions of their authors. The facts have been unduly qualified by the views which they are subsequently used to justify.

Now, the science of religions is at present in the position of all young sciences. Its accumulated phenomena are numerous and at the same time vastly incomplete; while the interpretations of them are various and, in the words of a high authority, speaking of one section only, 'so fundamentally opposed to each other that it seems impossible at present to take up a safe and well-founded position with regard to them [1].'

The Theist, then, is entitled to approach religious history with an initial presumption, provided that he do so with care. He believes in a Personal God; and the need of self-communication is part of what he means by personality. He believes that persons were created that God might hold

[1] O. Schrader.

intercourse with them and they with Him; prayer and its answer being two sides of one spiritual fact. Consequently, he expects to find religion universal, from the time that man first was man; and assumes that wherever its human manifestations occur, their divine counterpart must have been present also. This belief does not rest upon history, but upon his analysis of his own personality and religious experience; and he brings it with him, not as a disguised induction, but as an antecedent expectation, to the study of historical facts.

And here we are met at once by the supposed objection to religion which is drawn from the antiquity of man. The picture of man's slow evolution is by this time too familiar, and has been too often drawn to need repetition. Geology finds him existing at a date immensely earlier than had once been supposed; and though this date can only be relatively determined, its distance from the dawn of history would seem, on the most moderate computation, to have far exceeded that from the dawn of history to the present day. Further, he existed during this long prehistoric period in a rude and uncivilized condition, as regards his method and appliances of life. Biology has added the conjecture that his physical frame, at least, was developed from some lower animal form; and this, if true, as on the evidence seems to be extremely probable, would almost necessitate a still earlier date for his first appearance than we might otherwise have been disposed to accept. Now, there is no question but that a strong atheistic presumption is created in many minds by this spectacle of the long savagery of man. The religious world has long been accustomed to the existence of irreligion on its outskirts, and is not seriously perplexed by the fact. For, at any rate, the immense mass of mankind, throughout the whole historic period, have been within the reach of religious influence. Egypt, Babylon, China and the great Indo-European family have all possessed sufficient religion to justify the theistic belief that, amid multitudinous human errors, God left not Himself without witness. And, in comparison with these great races, the scattered savage tribes, who have seemed to know no God, are relatively insignificant in their effect upon the imagination. Their state has been accounted for by gradual moral degradation; and though the religious mind has been distressed by it, it has not been overwhelmed. But when the whole proportion and scale of these things is suddenly transformed, and savagery, instead of representing the mere fringe of failure round human progress, is represented as the normal condition of our race, during far the greater part of its existence, the result is a stupendous shock to all our preconceived ideas. It is plausibly urged that those, who were no more civilized than modern savages, can have possessed no better morality or religious belief; and the question forces itself upon us with importunate insistence, 'Can a race that has been left for such limitless ages to itself really have been the object of divine solicitude the while?' Even the survey of religious development within the historic period has prompted a Christian writer to ask, 'On the hypothesis that God had a gracious thought in His heart towards the human race . . . how can we imagine Him going about the execution of His plan for the good of humanity with such wearisome deliberation? . . . Is not the slow process too cold-blooded, so to speak, for the warm temperament of grace? . . . Is the slowness of the evolution not a proof that the alleged purpose is not a reality?[1]' And such obstinate questionings come over us with a thousandfold intensity as we gaze down the long vista of the prehistoric ages. They do not really constitute any logical difficulty; but they raise an imaginative presumption of considerable weight and force, which leads many minds to approach the history of religion with a strong anti-theistic predisposition.

Now, we must remember that the facts in question are for the most part absolutely neutral, while such positive indications as they give point rather in a religious direction. They are thus summarized by a popular writer whose bias is distinctly untheo-

[1] Dr. Bruce.

logical[1]: 'As regards religious ideas they can only be inferred from the relics buried with the dead, and these are scarce and uncertain for the earlier periods.... All we can say is that from the commencement of the Neolithic period downwards there is abundant proof that man had ideas of a future state of existence very similar to those of most of the savage tribes of the present day. Such proof is wanting for the immensely longer Palaeolithic period, and we are left to conjecture.' Moreover, prehistoric man was not precisely in the same situation as the modern savage. There is all the difference between them of first and second childhood. The one represents the remnant of humanity that has failed to progress; the other must have contained in himself the germ of all the progressive peoples. Even the implements and weapons, which with the one are archaic survivals, must have been original inventions with the other. The similarity of their external condition need not, therefore, indicate too close a similarity of capacity and character. A man may have high thoughts amidst very low surroundings; and the most meditative nations have not always been the most progressive—as witness 'the stationary East.' If, therefore, we believe, as we do, that a divine influence is distinctly traceable throughout the historic period, there is nothing whatever to suggest its

---

[1] S. Laing.

absence from the prehistoric races, and the presumption is in its favour. 'It matters little,' as M. Reville well says, 'that the dawn of the religious sentiment in the human soul may have been associated with simple and rude notions of the world and of the object of faith. The point of departure is fixed and the journey begins. In substance it comes to precisely the same thing to say, God revealed Himself in the beginning to man as soon as man had reached a certain stage in his psychic development, as to say Man was so constituted that, arrived at a certain stage in his psychic development, he must become sensible of the reality of the divine influence. In this sense ... we would accept the idea of a primitive revelation [1].'

Thus the picture of man's long infancy, which science has unrolled, in no way affects the reality of religion. It may modify our view of the method which God has pursued in His intercourse with men; but it contains nothing to shake our belief in the probability of that intercourse. And there is no need to be alarmed at what turns out, upon examination, to be no necessary verdict of facts, but only the old atheistic hypothesis read again into the new facts, without logical justification of any sort or form.

On passing from the prehistoric to the earliest historic ages, we are at once met by the broad distinction between *cultus* and mythology—that is

[1] Proleg. to *Philos. of Religion.*

to say, between ceremonies, institutions, usages, ritual observances on the one hand, and the reasons given for them, their intellectual explanation or justification on the other—what we should now call religious practice and religious belief. Recent research has paid special attention to the former of these two elements of ancient religion—the ceremonial, or customary—as being older than most recorded mythology, more popular in extent and origin, more persistently tenacious of life, and calculated, therefore, to throw more light upon the spiritual condition of the early world. Indeed this priority of custom to creed has been utilized by a recent German writer[1] in the service of a theory which would explain away religion, by representing it as an artificial endeavour to account for what at first was irrational habit. But the fact that the reasons assigned for an ancient custom are mutually inconsistent, and in some cases demonstrably untrue, is no proof whatever that the custom in question had no original reason at all. Habits may become irrational or instinctive, but they can hardly begin by being so; nor can any number of habits which have no religious foundation possibly originate religious ideas. And accordingly the theory in question has to fall back for further support upon the old notion that religion was at first an artificial invention; but this is only a survival

[1] Gruppe.

of those obsolete views of the last century, which regarded society in all its forms as artificial, and which modern historic science has discredited for ever. Such a paradox, therefore, however ingeniously defended, is not likely in the present day to do much harm; while it may be of some use in drawing attention to the basis of fact upon which it rests—the extreme importance of ritual conduct in early society. For instance, there was the worldwide institution of sacrifice, whether viewed as a feast of fellowship and communion between gods and men, or as a tribute, a propitiation, an atonement. There were annual and seasonal festivals, whose customs of long-forgotten meaning linger on into the world to-day. There were agricultural and pastoral sacraments connected with the firstfruits of the field or flock, the sources of many a surviving rustic superstition and quaint provincial phrase. Then there were all the observances attendant upon birth and death; ceremonies of initiation on adolescence; marriage customs; funeral rites; fastings, flagellations, penances; scrupulous systems of taboo; the solemnities of the kindling of fire, of the drawing of water, of the felling of trees. These and other occasions and actions, too many and various to enumerate, were matters of ritual regulation, in which time, place, condition of body, posture, gesture, language, dress were minutely and carefully prescribed. Much of this customary religion, of course, coincides with historic periods; but its prevalence can be inferred from early literature and folk-lore far beyond the horizon of recorded history. It has all the marks of immemorial age about it, and may well have dated from primeval man.

'Political institutions are older than political theories, and in like manner religious institutions are older than religious theories . . . ritual and practical usage were, strictly speaking, the sum total of ancient religions. Religion in primitive times was not a system of belief with practical applications; it was a body of fixed traditional practices to which every member of society conformed as a matter of course. . . . A man was born into a fixed relation to certain gods as surely as he was born into relation to his fellow-men; and his religion—that is, the part of conduct which was determined by his relation to the gods—was simply one side of the general scheme of conduct prescribed for him by his position as a member of society. There was no separation between the sphere of religious and of ordinary life. Every social act had a reference to the gods as well as to men, for the social body was not made up of men only, but of gods and men: . . . in every region of the world, as soon as we find a nation or tribe emerging from prehistoric darkness into the light of authentic history we find also that its religion conforms to the general type which has just been indicated[1].'

What was the dominant tone of this early religion? 'The severe aspect of natural religion,' says Dr. Newman, in a well-known place, 'is the most prominent aspect.' It is not 'a satisfaction or refuge, but a terror and a superstition.' 'Its large and deep foundation is the sense of sin and guilt.' And again, 'wherever religion exists in a popular shape, it has almost invariably worn its dark side outwards[2].' This view, for which Lucretius is continually quoted—Lucretius, the avowed enemy of all religion—is without doubt an overstatement of the case. And Professor Robertson Smith is as much in accordance with the facts as we now know them when he says, 'The identity of religious occasions and festal seasons may be taken as the determining characteristic of the type of ancient religion generally[3].' But the whole situation is best described by M. Reville: 'Let us never forget,' he says, 'that whatever might be the notion which he formed in his own mind of the divinity, man has always experienced and cherished a special sense of comfort in being in normal relation with it, and that even when this divinity presented itself to him under terrifying aspects. . . . In the religious sentiment the sentiment of dependence is intimately

---

[1] Robertson Smith, *Religion of Semites.*
[2] *Grammar of Assent.*   [3] *Religion of Semites.*

mingled with the sentiment of union, of reciprocity and of mutuality, which is no less essential to religion than the former. We may see here a double gamut or a double series of sentiments ...

respect, veneration, fear, dismay, terror:
admiration, joy, confidence, love, extasy.

The two gamuts—one of which has fear for its fundamental tone, and the other confidence—are most frequently mingled in reality. It is sometimes one which prevails and sometimes the other, but with an infinite variety of shades, of half-tones, and, if we may say so, of quarter-tones[1].' Much of this customary religion, when examined in detail, is crude, blundering, irrational; and its long dominion can hardly fail to suggest similar misgivings to those which we have considered in connexion with the antiquity of the race. But one fact stands out from it with startling prominence — the powerful, the tremendous hold of religion upon man. It is coextensive with his conduct, about his path and about his bed. He cannot shake it off. It comforts him, it controls him; it is natural, it is normal. He may feel himself to be now in fellowship with, now in alienation from his gods. But in either case he takes for granted a divine interest in his affairs; a response to his acts and aspirations from the divine side; a divine desire for communication and communion

[1] Proleg. to *Philos. of Religion*.

with himself. It may be granted that the intellectual conceptions which accompanied all this were of the vaguest. At a time when man had no clear notion of his own personality, as distinct from nature on the one hand, and from his family and tribe on the other, the outlines also of the supernatural and superhuman would be indistinct. But it is precisely this indistinctness which gives its evidential value to early religion. Man did not know what to think of it, stammered in the effort to explain it, and yet allowed it to bind him hand and foot. There was a reality about it which he could not, a necessity which he would not, evade. A power grasped him, and grasped him for his good. Now, that power ultimately rested either upon a fiction or a truth. However beneficial in operation, it was in its last analysis a lie, or it was God, amid and despite of superstition and ignorance and error, claiming men's allegiance in the only manner and degree in which, at that particular stage of his development, it could be claimed.

If there were no organic continuity in history, and the past were separated from the present by a gulf, this dilemma might remain unsolved. But the power in question is an earlier form of, and essentially identical with, the power of religion as we see it in the world to-day. We are, therefore, entitled to judge it by what it has become. As existing in the far past we can only view it from outside; but as existing in the present we can view it also from within. And if the result of that inner acquaintance with religion has been to convince us of its truth, we may logically extend the conviction to its every bygone phase. The early prevalence of customary religion, with its subordination of creed to conduct, will then become additional evidence of its providential origin—as initiating with irresistible power a course of spiritual development, which its subjects at the time could neither foresee nor understand

To say this is not to force a fanciful theory upon the facts: it is merely to assert that those facts are more intelligible upon our own than upon any adverse theory. Historic science discovers facts which when once discovered are common property. And we are manifestly within our rights when we claim that the facts of early religion are far less compatible with its falsehood than with its truth; its crudity being no more than we should antecedently expect, while its hold upon life was too powerful and purposeful to be other than divine.

But however clearly it may be established that sacrifices, and observances, and rites of a religious nature preceded the great mass of recorded mythology, they still presuppose some kind of elementary religious belief; and the question again arises, Are the earlier forms of religious belief compatible with the thought of revelation? Three views of the case are possible. There is, first, the theory of a clear monotheistic revelation to primitive man, which was subsequently lost by the majority of our race, and whose dim and distorted fragments, floating mist-like over the earth, have given rise to the various mythologies. This theory, though it has met with a certain amount of scientific support, was probably theological in origin; being closely connected with that view of history which was once thought to be contained in Genesis; but which, at any rate, we English, as Professor Maurice pointed out, owe far more directly and immediately to Milton[1]. It cannot be better summarized than in the words of Doctor South[2]: 'Adam,' he says, 'came into the world a philosopher'; and again, 'Aristotle was but the rubbish of an Adam.' We have only to compare such statements with the opening chapters of Genesis, to see at once how much arbitrary assumption they import into the text. The very form of the account in Genesis is too obviously Oriental and mythical to be pressed into history, in the Western sense of the word; while even as it stands it involves no one view more than another of the nature of primeval revelation. Its spiritual analysis of man is profoundly and eternally true, but is as compatible with a low as with a high state of

---

[1] See note 21.
[2] Qu. in Maurice, *Moral and Metaphys. Philos.* ii.

intellect and culture; and while it asserts the fact of divine intercourse with the human conscience, it cannot be said to indicate its method—

> 'Whether of actual vision, sensible
> To sight and feeling, or that in this sort
> Have condescendingly been shadowed forth
> Communications spiritually maintained
> And intuitions moral and divine[1].'

Nor has the theory in question more scientific than Scriptural support. It has, indeed, been maintained that the earlier stages of the chief historic religions are more monotheistic than the later, and point, therefore, to an original monotheism behind them. But the language in which these early monotheistic tendencies are clothed, is too obviously rooted in more primitive modes of thought to admit of such an interpretation. It has all the air of a growth and not a reminiscence; a development, not a degradation. And, further, there are, imbedded in religious literature and popular folk-lore, fossil fragments of earlier and cruder mythological formations, which would seem in all cases to have preceded the purer forms of the great historic religions.

Hence has arisen the extreme converse of the above theory—the view that the world's theology began with the crudest and most childlike conceptions, such as are to be found among the lower

[1] Wordsworth, *Excursion*.

savages of the present day, and was thence gradually refined and developed to the high level which we find in the Vedas and Avesta, and in the earlier religion of Egypt. The details of this theory, full of interest as they are, have by this time become too familiar to need repetition. At the same time they have hitherto usually been represented as arguments against the reality of any revelation. But all that they could really disprove, if true, are hypotheses like that above mentioned, as to the method which a divine revelation has or ought to have pursued. When, however, we bear in mind the great law of education through illusion, to which we referred above, and also the frequent coexistence of strong personal religion with crude theology, we can easily believe that, if man was developed from a state of complete savagery, God may have revealed Himself to him by correspondingly slow degrees, and through appropriately limited intellectual conceptions, and yet all the while with sufficient certainty to make some degree of spiritual life possible.

> 'And those illusions which excite the scorn
> Or, more, the pity of unthinking minds—
> Are they not mainly outward ministers
> Of inward conscience?—with whose service charged
> They came, and go, appeared, and disappear,
> Diverting evil purposes, remorse
> Awakening, chastening an intemperate grief,
> Or pride of heart abating [1].'

[1] Wordsworth, *Excursion*.

But this extreme theory, if true, is as yet very far indeed from demonstration. There is an undue simplicity about it; and all attempts to arrange human progress in stages, whether empirically determined as by Comte, or rationally as by Hegel, have split upon this rock; they are inadequate to the subtlety and complexity of nature. As a matter of fact, mythology has been evolved from many sources—necessities of language, diseases of language, stupid mistakes of language, poetry, speculation, story-telling, priestcraft, inspired visions and immoral dreams. It is partly a natural growth, partly an artificial invention, partly the result of conscious or unconscious borrowing from one race by another. And it is a mistake to suppose that as a whole it was ever very closely connected with religion, even when we find it woven round the names and histories of gods. In the Homeric poems, for instance, a broad distinction may be palpably felt between the implied religion and the expressed mythology; a high and pure and simple and natural religious tone, such as could never either have been suggested or sustained by the celestial romance with which, nevertheless, it is inextricably interwoven. There are many similar cases in religious literature; and we may well believe, therefore, that in ruder ages a like difference existed, between the inner feeling which accompanied the prayer or rite or sacrifice, and the weird fetichistic or totemistic fancies by which it was often overlaid; and that then too, as so often since, the heart was nearer heaven than the head. If so, we might adopt an intermediate view between the two above-mentioned extremes, to the effect that God did first reveal Himself to the mind of man, under such simple mythical forms as seem to be necessitated by the very nature of early language and thought, but with sufficient clearness to make those myths an inspiring, ennobling, elevating influence, the beginning of a real religious bond between the human and divine. After all, the great natural sacraments of the evening and the dawn must have had something of the same strange spiritual attraction for the earliest man that they still have for us, with all our scientific knowledge of how their witchery is wrought; and love and death, the two great twin teachers, must have been as potent then as now to strain the human heart with yearning towards the mysterious sunset land. The hypothesis that these higher stages of natural religion were only reached after an age-long worship of stocks, and stones, and 'four-footed beasts, and creeping things,' is hardly so probable as the Pauline view, that the exact converse was the case. If the first of our two previously-mentioned theories overestimated the action of degeneracy, the second certainly very much underrates it. The moral and spiritual degeneration of races is an important fact in history, and acts immediately upon the religious conceptions; and we may safely infer that it was equally active in prehistoric ages. And consequently when we meet with petty, grotesque, absurd, obscene, horrible objects and forms of worship, there is a reasonable presumption that they are largely due, not to original limitation of intellect, but to gradual moral deterioration and distortion. An intermediate view, therefore, which regards man's original conceptions, as neither so high nor yet so low as is sometimes apt to be supposed, accords most nearly with the facts of comparative mythology as we at present know them; while it still leaves a wide margin, within which different minds will continue to differ, unless fresh facts ever throw a materially new light upon the subject. Thus myth, but not unmoral or ignoble myth, would seem to have been man's first fashion of thinking about God—such myth as primeval thought and language would inevitably suggest, in speaking of the storms and seasons, the sun, the moon, the stars; and if so, myth may be regarded as God's first instrument of revelation to the mind, as distinct from the conscience and the heart of man. 'He left not Himself without witness.'

Thus the survey of the subhistoric age, the age of myth and custom, presents us with precisely such a picture of religion as we should expect after discovering the antiquity of man—a religion which, though rudimentary, is recognizably real, since it is a link in a continuous chain, an inseparable part of a progressive system, whose later phases we have stronger reason for regarding as revealed.

Christians, it should be remembered, from the days of Tertullian and Clement of Alexandria, have always been accustomed to take two broadly different views of the pre-Christian religions of the world; views which may be called respectively the polemical and the philosophic; the one concerned with the falsehood in them, needing contradiction, the other with their relative truth, as preparing the way for higher things. The contrast may be well illustrated by a comparison of Milton's treatment of the heathen gods in *Paradise Lost*, with that of Wordsworth in the fourth book of the *Excursion*. The natural tendency of our modern historic method, and our increased knowledge of the world's sacred literature, has been to emphasize the latter, the Alexandrian, the Wordsworthian point of view. For no reader of the Vedas or the Avesta, the Accadian psalms or the Egyptian ritual of the dead, can fail to recognize in them the true ring of real religion. And the old form of apology, therefore, which endeavoured to establish the truth of Christianity by contrasting it with the falsehood of all previous creeds, has for us become a thing of the past. It lingers indeed still in certain quarters, but is no longer really tenable; as being not only

M

contradicted by the obvious facts of history, but also in its very nature suicidal, since it seeks to enhance the importance of a special revelation by discrediting the natural religion, to which such a revelation must appeal; to elevate the superstructure by destroying its foundation[1]. But all reactions may be carried too far, and we are perhaps in some danger at the present moment of over-facile acquiescence in doctrines of consistent religious progress. Progress there has undoubtedly been in the history of religion, but of a kind that is more easily felt than defined. To begin with, there is, as we have seen, no uniform agreement among authorities as regards its precise level of departure: nor can there be any more as to its goal, since an Agnostic, a Theist, and a Christian, with their different standards of religious perfection, must have different criteria of progress. Again, many of the dates, which would have an important bearing upon the relative priority of different systems, are at present unascertained, and perhaps for ever unascertainable. And then, too, the effect of degeneration is a wholly undefinable quantity, on which the widest variety of opinion will continue to exist. All these are considerations which should qualify our acceptance of glib generalities about religious evolution. Moreover, a still more important point to bear in mind is the distinction, pre-

[1] See note 22.

viously noticed, between what we should now call personal religion and theology. We are very apt to overestimate, as a source of evidence, what may be called the external element in early religion, from the fact that it has survived in literature, ritual and folk-lore, and consequently been handed down to us; while the personal religion which underlay it has passed unrecorded away. We read of seven thousand opponents of Baal-worship in Israel, when the eye of the contemporary prophet could see none. And the case is typical. There was domestic piety in the Rome of Juvenal, and Christian life in the ninth and tenth centuries, those dark ages of the Church. And it must have been so throughout all religious history. We continually find among the uneducated poor of the present day an amount of religion which controls, comforts, and refines their whole life, combined with few theological conceptions, and those often of the crudest; while the most religious minds among the educated and cultured classes are the most acutely conscious of the inadequacy of language to portray the object of their faith; and the highest personal religion always tends to mysticism, a sense of spiritual communion which 'lies all too deep for words.' But it is precisely by the extent and intensity of this hidden life, the number whom it affects, and the degree in which it affects them, that the real vitality of a religion should be judged; while judgement is further complicated by the fact that spiritual revivals often tend to recur to archaic methods of expression, and present therefore to the eye of history an illusory appearance of retrogression. Of the two main factors of religion, therefore, we can only deal with the more external, that is the mythological and ritual remains. And this fact seriously detracts from the completeness of any generalizations that may be made on the nature and character of religious progress. We can gauge the intellect, but not the spirit of the distant past, and it is to the spirit that revelation is made. Separate races seem to have been dominated by separate elements of religious thought, each having its special type, its characteristic idea; but the isolation of these elements has been much qualified in popular practice, and by an easy reaction has passed over into its opposite, leaving a general impression of fluctuation rather than of progress upon the mind; while ritual has been substantially identical the whole world over, and has persisted, with but little change, through successive refinements of interpretation, reformations of religion, changes of creed. But all these things tell us nothing of the inner hopes and fears, amid which, one by one, men lived and died.

In brief, then, we must remember that the science of religions has only a partial access to the phenomena with which it deals; and, further, that it is still in the empirical stage, most of its generalizations being as yet more or less hypothetical, and needing careful scrutiny before they can become premisses, from which further conclusions may be drawn.

LECTURE VII

RELIGION IN PRE-CHRISTIAN HISTORY

WHEN we pass from the more or less conjectural reconstruction of primitive religion to the great historic creeds, we are at once on more accessible and more familiar ground. From the moment of their entry upon our horizon, the historic nations of the world are in possession of definite religions, which, though distinguished by many local and racial peculiarities, contain much that is common property, both in modes of thought and ways of worship. These religions have had to encounter various disintegrating forces, patronage, persecution, popular degradation and distortion, schismatic disruption, infidel attack. Yet however modified, they have persisted with a tenacious vitality, that abundantly proves how natural religion is to man. He cannot get rid of it, do what he will.

Now we have already seen the apologetic value of this universality of religion, as creating a presumption of its truth. But that apologetic value would be seriously impaired if we did not believe that all religion had its divine counterpart or element of inspiration from on high. Consequently there can be no greater mistake—from an apologetic point of view—than to depreciate the ethnic religions in the supposed interests of an exclusive revelation. For if it were granted that the majority of the religions in the world had existed unsustained by any kind of inspiration, this would constitute a strong presumption that the remainder were in similar case. The world's religion is too much of a piece to be torn asunder in this way. There is too obvious a solidarity about it. Its higher stages are inseparably joined with the lower steps that have led up to them; and if we held that the mass of mankind had been deceived in supposing themselves capable of intercourse with the spiritual world, we should have no logical right to make a particular exception. Of course this implies the existence of degrees of inspiration or revelation; but that is neither a new thought, nor one likely to be denied in an age whose characteristic category is development. It was the absence of the notion of development, and therefore of degrees of inspiration which involved the Gnostics in all their difficulties about the Old Testament. For conceiving that the morality of all its characters, and the obvious anthropomorphism of its language were to be judged by the highest

Christian standard, they had no alternative but to reject the Old Testament altogether. Origen saw in what direction the true answer to this must lie, though he did not dwell on it at length. But for us the notion of a relative and gradual revelation to the Hebrew race has become a commonplace. And it is natural that the same principle should extend to all other religions. We have already seen, within the limits of the individual life, how gradual the process of God's self-revelation is, and how dependent upon character and conduct, even when what may be called its external instruments lie ready to hand, in the shape of a theology and ethic refined by the highest religious tradition. Consequently we should still more expect this to be the case, under the less favourable circumstances of a time, when divine personality could not be conceived except in terms of polytheism, nor divine omnipresence except in terms of pantheism, nor divine holiness except in terms of dualism, or in the earlier ages for which even such terms as these were too advanced. And what is true of the individual must be equally true of the individual 'writ large' in the family, the class, the tribe, the nation, the race.

We expect, then, *a priori*, that wherever there is religion there will be notes of inspiration or revelation about it; but we are very far from expecting that these notes will be invariably clear.

And on turning to religious history this is what seems to be the case. The picture is a confused one, and patient of various interpretations, while every increase in our knowledge of its details makes generalization less secure; each path ends as we pursue it, each clue fails as we follow it up. There is evidence enough on all sides of man seeking God, if haply he might find Him, but far less of God finding or being found of man. Still superficial views of history are seldom accurate, especially where the things of the spirit are concerned. Isolated events should no more be expected to reveal God than isolated atoms, abstract history than abstract matter. And in the present case there will be found much which, on reflection, tends to qualify our initial disappointment.

To begin with, there is the actual hold of religion upon man, its grasp of him. We have already considered this in relation to uncivilized races, but it is no less evident elsewhere. The ritual regulations of India, Persia, Babylon, Egypt, speak for themselves. They are obviously human enough; minute, excessive, often puerile. Yet there is something behind them; they labour to formulate something other than themselves, a power, an order, an authority, of which man is vaguely but really conscious, and which he craves to have translated into words that he can understand. We turn with impatience from the endless pages of the religious law-books of the world; but their very mass is an indication of the divine superintendence which they symbolize; an effort to express the sense of infinite obligation, by the accumulation of infinitesimal rules.

Again, there is what may be called the internal evidence of the world's religious literature, the intellectual illumination, the high moral precepts, the flashes of spiritual insight which it contains. The proportion of these things has been often exaggerated by detachment of them from their context, their common-place, wearisome, even offensive context. They are rare gems in an earthy matrix; dust of gold in a base alloy. But still there they are. The fact of them remains, and must be taken into account. By themselves, indeed, they would hardly convey the inspiration of their utterers or authors to a mind otherwise indisposed to believe it, and might easily be attributed to what is commonly called unassisted or natural reason. But they are parts of a whole, and help to link the lower and more human seeming creeds, to those of whose divine origination there is other and stronger proof; thus emphasizing the ultimate unity of religion, as well as its universality, and suggesting the presence in its earlier phases of the same Spirit that has guided its mature results.

Then, again, there is the extensive belief in one

kind or another of divine intercourse with man. From the savage who is not yet consciously separated from his crudely conceived divinities, to the saint who is in conscious reunion with a holy God, man has taken his religious relationships as facts. That is to say, he has not only regarded himself as related to God, but God, in one way or another, as related to himself, and this has naturally led to the recognition of inspiration or revelation. Its organs have been various. Now the king, now the sage, now the bard, the ascetic, the prophet, or the priest, has been viewed as the favourite recipient of communications from on high; but the fact of the communications has remained undoubted, and has powerfully influenced life. Of course it is easy enough to set such things aside as hallucinations, the older theory of imposture being somewhat out of date. But as our knowledge of their power and prevalence increases, this can hardly be done without involving our whole 'rational make and constitution' in the same suspicion—a *reductio ad absurdum*, which will give most men pause. While for all who do not deny its possibility in this arbitrary way, the existence of the belief in question is a fact of weight; for it would hardly have maintained its hold upon our race throughout the ages, unless verified in ways and degrees that we can better guess than gauge. For it is the old, we must remember, and not the young, who transmit the traditions of religion; those, that is, who have acquired assurance by the inner experience of a lifetime, and can add the comment of their own conviction to the text. And the value of this conviction cannot possibly be tested by the mere amount of evidence now producible to us; the slender basis on which, as seen down the long historical perspective, it appears to us to rest. For it is in the colour and complexion of that evidence to contemporary eyes, its spiritual complement in the hearts and consciences of those to whom it first appealed that all its real cogency consists. And with this in mind, we may fairly assert that the antiquity, the persistence, the continuous transmission of man's belief in some sort of revelation, inspiration, or other intercourse with God is a powerful corroboration of its truth[1].

Thus the picture of the world's religion as a whole impresses us with a conviction which it is difficult to analyze, but difficult also to resist. Infinite ingenuity has been expended in explaining it away, but with infinitesimal result. It is so universal, its fundamental principles so similar, its hold upon human life so strong, its influence upon human history so incalculably great, that we cannot believe there is nothing real behind it, and the alternative to nothing is God; 'God working far more deliberately, far more obscurely, than we

[1] See note 23.

might have expected, yet indicating perhaps by that very fact that He is God.

This much at least might be said if the ethnic religions stood alone; but they do not stand alone. There is the Hebrew religion. The Hebrew Scriptures are a part of the religious literature of the world, and are linked and connected with the remainder of that literature by countless analogies of thought and form. Whatever further light, therefore, the Old Testament throws upon religion, must be used in the interpretation of all inferior forms of belief; while they in turn, as, in that light, their drift and meaning gather clearness, illustrate the development of the creed which is their crown, and in so doing assist the argument—the cumulative argument—for the common element of truth which they contain. In saying this, one is taking for granted, what no competent student is ever likely to deny; that our increased acquaintance with the religious literature of the ancient world has emphasized the supremacy of the Old Testament Scriptures. They still stand in lonely eminence, as they have always stood, immeasurably superior to all else of their kind.

Now of the two elements which may be broadly distinguished in the Old Testament, the prophetic and the priestly, it is the former which gives its peculiar, its unique character, to the book. The priestly element closely resembles much that we meet elsewhere; but the prophetic at once differentiates Hebrew religion, and Hebrew history from that of the remainder of the world, and has always constituted one of the strongest special arguments for belief in a personal God.

Hebrew prophecy has two aspects, its ultimate and its contemporary aspect. Its ultimate aspect, when viewed as a whole, is that of a preparation for the Incarnation. As such it had immense weight in the earlier days of Christianity, and is of immense weight still. For though the modern tendency is to limit the vision of the individual prophets, every step in this direction of necessity increases our conviction of their providential superintendence. But this aspect of Hebrew prophecy only affects our present subject indirectly, through its connexion with Christian belief. It is otherwise with its contemporary aspect. That has an immediate bearing on divine personality, as presenting us with direct evidence of divine inspiration. Here, too, in modern days, we have somewhat changed our point of view; but in a constructive, not a destructive, direction. The change in fact resembles, and strictly speaking is a part of, our changed attitude towards the argument from final causes or design in nature, of which design in history is at once the corollary and crown.

The character of this change has been already pointed out. There was a tendency, when design was first observed in nature, to regard every object in the world as having a definite final cause; a particular purpose or function which it was destined to subserve; an end outside itself. This was what is called a mechanical teleology, or teleology which viewed the world as a machine. It was inadequate, and like all inadequate conceptions partly false; but at the same time it was an inevitable stage in the development of our modern organic teleology.

We now recognize that a fuller and more complete view of nature is to be obtained, by looking at things as in the first instance ends in themselves, organisms destined to exist and to preserve and perpetuate their own existence; and, incidentally, as it were, in so doing to fulfil other and further purposes 'in that eternal circle life pursues.'

Now the argument from prophecy was at one time presented as an argument from design of the narrower sort. The prophets were regarded as specially inspired to predict future events. The prediction of the future was in fact their final cause, and the fulfilment of the prediction, the proof of their inspiration. But the progress of criticism has modified this view, by showing how many political and social predictions of the prophets were never in any literal sense fulfilled at all; and has further called attention to the fact, that the recorded fulfilment of a prediction in the past depends for its value upon the date of the record, and as long as that is an open, or doubtful question, cannot reasonably be used in controversial argument.

This criticism has led us to look closer at the prophets, and resulted in a deeper insight into their character and work. We now recognize that the primary mission of a prophet is to his age. He is a preacher of righteousness to the men of his day. His sufficient reason is there and then. But righteousness may be preached in many ways. And the Hebrew prophets are distinguished by their conviction that righteousness is the will of an omnipotent Person, the Creator of the material as well as of the moral universe; consequently that sooner or later, it must work itself out in the material world, it must make the material world its own, it must triumph visibly.

Thus their insight into the moral law enabled them to predict, as the insight into physical law enables a man of science to predict. Such prophecy must be distinguished from the minute and detailed prediction of historic times, and seasons, and persons and events. With the latter, and the countless controversies in which it is involved, our present inquiry has no concern. If universally true, such predictions cannot be logically verified, and therefore would not assist our argument. If frequently false they would only illustrate the human fallibility of the prophets, which we do not for a moment deny, and in so doing would emphasize the superhuman origin of their central thought—the inevitable triumph of divine righteousness in the world. This is their eternal prophecy; and however distant its complete realization, every age has seen it partially fulfilled. Thus, in speaking to their own, the prophets spoke to other ages. Primarily they preached; incidentally they prophesied; because they proclaimed a law which operates in ever-widening circles. And though the fulfilment of prediction, thus understood, may seem to many minds less evidential than the apposite occurrence of a name or date would be, it carries with it a more profound conviction that we have reached the spiritual heart of things, and are in presence of the Power that moves the world. Nor is this view of prophecy so novel as is sometimes supposed. For, paradoxical as the statement may seem, it rests on the same principle as that mystical interpretation which has always had a place in the Christian Church. Mystical interpretation, as applied by its real masters, was no mere play of poetic fancy, no arbitrary reading into history or prophecy of a meaning which it did not contain. It rested upon the principle that all true spiritual utterances, or spiritually circumstanced events, are manifestations of a law which is eternal; and may therefore be regarded as symbolic or descriptive of every subsequent operation of that law; while since history deepens as it develops, deepens in complexity and scope, its later phases express more fully what its earlier did but indicate, and in this sense are the realities of which the latter were the types.

But though this method of interpretation is true in principle, its prevalence has tended to obscure the facts of history from many minds. The literal and the mystical fulfilment of prophecy have become confused. And absorbed in the thought of its spiritual realization, men have lost sight of its innumerable historic failures. The prophets have been regarded as infallible oracles, and thereby emptied of their true humanity. Whereas it is precisely in their true humanity that their significance consists. They were not only liable to faint and fail like other men, but also to err in their practical application of that spiritual truth which they possessed. They were akin to the religious leaders of all other races; they were men and not machines. And it is their common humanity which throws their exceptional character into such relief. They are a series of men, ' of like passions with ourselves,' in whom the conviction of intercourse with God reached its climax and complete expression. As a result of this intercourse they proclaim the unity and holiness of God, in accents of unfaltering certitude. 'Thus saith the Lord,' is their continual cry. In other words, they believe themselves inspired. Further, they recognize their own inspiration, and its necessary revelation to their people, as constituting a mission, a destiny, a call ; first to separate themselves from other nations, and then to proclaim, to other nations, the truth which they alone possess. They thus progressively shape a people and compose a literature, penetrated by monotheism, and by the certainty of its ultimate triumph in the world; the latter thought, as we have seen, of necessity flowing from the former, as its inevitable consequence when consistently thought out. Thus the prophets have a place of their own in the history of the world. Their existence and their immediate work are unaffected by critical controversies. They stand out among the greatest of our race. We have seen that the whole human race has tended to believe in personal gods, and in the possibility of intercourse with them ; and that the higher degrees of that intercourse, by the common consent of every nation, have been attributed only to the few; while the few in divers degrees have professed its experience and transmitted its tradition. It is in the company of these few, though eminent above them, that the Hebrew prophets stand. And this must be borne in mind, in weighing their witness to our belief in God. However abnormal their experience, it was of a kind which the human race expected, and for which it everywhere and always looked. It has the instinct of all humanity behind it, and is strengthened by that instinct, while it strengthens it in turn. Now the prophets claim inspiration; they profess their conviction that God is personally speaking through them. They exhibit the natural human concomitants of such a condition. They shrink back, they are abashed, they despond, they fly, they agonize at the greatness of their fate. And yet when they speak, they speak with the serene authority of certitude. They are disinterested; they have nothing to gain and all to lose by their vocation. They are sane; there is no morbid phrensy or fanatical excitement about them. They proclaim a truth which they are sure by its very nature must prevail. And in fact it has prevailed. This is their great, their world-wide, their undeniable fulfilment. And the significance of it cannot, for our purpose, be more decisively expressed than by quoting its most uncompromising critic. 'What,' asks Professor Kuenen, 'did the Israelitish prophets accomplish? What was the result of their work, and what value are we to assign to it?'

Ethical monotheism is their creation. They have themselves ascended to the belief in one, only, holy, and righteous God, who realizes His will, or moral good, in the world, and they have, by preaching and writing, made that belief the inalienable property of our race[1].'

[1] *Prophets of Israel.*

What then are we to think of the psychological phenomenon which these men present? An opponent who, in the face of all the other lines of evidence, still disbelieves in a personal God, may perhaps not find much additional difficulty in regarding the prophets as deluded; though by so doing he will be landed in the awkward position, to which we have already had occasion to refer, of attributing a predominant factor in human progress, and by implication human progress itself, to a delusion. But, on the other hand, if we approach the prophets with the opposite presumption, we cannot but feel that they confirm our belief. They claim inspiration; it is a claim which, as we have seen, the majority of mankind has never thought unnatural. They claim an experience which, if true, is by that very fact above and beyond the power of any other men to analyse. And in virtue of this claim they have accomplished in the world, precisely what they professed themselves commissioned to accomplish. The simplest hypothesis about them is that they spoke the truth, and are a crowning evidence of God's personal intercourse with men.

But the significance of the prophets does not end here. The Old Testament, the prophetic book, remains; and when we speak of its inspiration, we do not merely mean that it was once inspired, but that it is still inspired as a present, an ever-present fact, which admits of experimental verification to-day. As there is a vague apprehension in many minds that modern criticism, in questioning our traditional views of the Bible, may invalidate its claim to inspiration, it is necessary that we should distinguish clearly between criticism and spiritual interpretation. Literary criticism—using the phrase in its most comprehensive sense;—literary criticism is a science, and its object is to find out facts; as for example, when, where and by whom a book was written; what precise words its author used, and what precise meaning he intended to convey. Its problems are complex; its methods subtle and somewhat subjective; many of its conclusions, at present, tentative. But it is a perfectly legitimate science, with a profoundly important end in view; and ought no more to be discredited than any other science, by the fact that its various exponents are not all equally wise, nor always in mutual accord. This science investigates the Bible, as it investigates the Avesta or the Vedas, and is as supreme within its province as it is impotent beyond. But inspiration is a phenomenon wholly and entirely beyond its province; a spiritual voice which can only be heard by the spiritual ear. The words and events of the Bible are its material medium of expression, its human organ of utterance; but when none are listening, they resemble a silent instrument of music, which may be handled, examined, criticized, classified, explained without thought of its latent power to stir the soul. Thus criticism and inspiration do not move in the same plane, and can never meet or interfere with one another, and the notion that they do so is due to a confusion of thought, from which the more polemical partisans of neither are quite free. In one case, indeed, this mistake may command our sympathy, though not our approval; in the case of the really religious man, who has come to associate spiritual truth with the particular form of thought, or words, in which it has habitually come home to himself, and sensitively shrinks from any severance of the two, as from the disruption of his very soul. Yet, however natural, this is a weakness, and a weakness in whose conquest the essence of spiritual progress oftentimes consists. Meanwhile, the existence of such men is a cloke for the far larger and less earnest class, whose religion consists in holding fast the form of sound words without its substance; the religious materialists of all time, who, knowing nothing of the interior life of the spirit, imagine that in grasping its externals they grasp all; and are proportionably alarmed at the very notion of examining what, with only too sure an instinct, they call the grounds of their belief. These men in turn play into the hands of the open opponents of all inspiration, by so intimately amalgamating the letter and the spirit that every criticism of the one shall seem a disparagement of the other, and thus enabling the results—the legitimate results of critical science—to be adroitly and plausibly misused for an illegitimate end.

The result of this misapplication of criticism on the one side, and of the nervous alarm which at once dreads it and yet contributes to cause it on the other, is to obscure the unassailable strength of the primary evidence for inspiration. For the highest evidence is self-evidence, which is independent of proof or demonstration from without. In the case of those abstract truths, like the mathematical axioms, which we intuitively recognize as soon as they are stated, this is obvious. But it holds equally good of concrete truths, or facts, of immediate experience. Our belief in the reality of an object, which we see before our eyes, can neither be diminished nor increased by argument. Our perception of beauty cannot be heightened by analysis, or qualified by explanation. Our conviction of an intimate friend's goodness is wholly independent of what other men may say of him in praise or blame. And it is upon such evidence that our belief in inspiration ultimately rests. Tradition may teach it, or criticism commend it, or authority command it; but experience, personal experience, can alone assure us of its truth. Such experience may take various forms, and pass through various degrees. We may begin by being struck with the spiritual power of the Old Testament, as contrasted with the other literature of the world; and then with its unity of tone, through all diversity of composition, its wonderful transcendence of the local and temporary elements that make it up; and then with its universality, its penetrating comprehension of every phase and condition of life. Thoughts of this kind will, in their turn, be confirmed and intensified, when we proceed to use the Bible in the conduct of our life, by its minute, its marvellous applicability to our every secret need; while now and again we are arrested, as with a lightning-flash, by sudden personal addresses of consolation or of warning that almost seem to rise into articulate speech.

What we have had occasion to say already of the argument from experience in general applies, of course, equally to this experience in particular. It is incommunicable, and we can no more reason from it, with those who do not possess it, than reason from music with the deaf, or from colour with the blind. But at least we may make our meaning clear, and insist that the argument in question shall not be deprived of its due weight, either by misunderstanding or misrepresentation. Belief in the inspiration of the Bible may mean no more than the acceptance of a tradition on authority; like belief in a scientific statement that we cannot personally verify. But we mean more by the phrase than this, when we use it as one of our reasons for faith in a personal God. We then mean that, whatever influence may have led us to the Bible, we have personally verified its claim, at least in one of the degrees above described; further, that we have witnessed that verification in others; and further, that with this double evidence before us, we are certain that such verification has gone on in every age, and given life to the authoritative tradition which has handed the Bible on. This is a fact of human history which cannot complacently be set aside; and a fact which, strong as it is in itself, becomes incalculably stronger, when taken in the cumulative context of the other lines of evidence, philosophical, historical and moral, that all converge upon the selfsame point.

Any criticism of the human element in the Bible, which makes it more truly human, more analogous with the workings of the human spirit other-where, tends without question to enhance our sense of its reality and worth. But even if the very converse were the case, and such criticism were really destructive, its only effect would be to throw this fact of spiritual power into stronger relief.

Spiritual truths are always immeasurably greater than their vehicles of utterance, and are often best expressed where this disproportion is most clearly seen. More than half the force of language consists in its associations; the hints, the side-lights, the suggestions, which its words do not imply, yet habitually convey. And language itself is often a far less adequate medium of expression than many inarticulate things; sighs, smiles, tears, glances, gestures, sacraments, symbols, signs. And

> 'truth in closest words shall fail,
> When truth embodied in a tale
> Shall enter in at lowly doors.'

This has always been notoriously the case with the Bible. Its power over the peasant is not diminished by his ignorance, nor its power over the scholar increased by his knowledge; for it is independent of the region in which ignorance and knowledge disagree. It flashes on the soul, through distorted or through clear conceptions; and in either case with equal ease. Doubtless when it spoke to Jerome and Augustine, its grammar and its history were less known than now. But it speaks to the modern student, of spiritual things, with neither increased nor diminished force. And this power in the Bible, which its believers attribute to inspiration, is a phenomenon that cannot otherwise be easily explained.

Further, this train of thought will throw a reflex light upon the other sacred books of the world. With all their imperfection and manifest inferiority, there is that in them which we can well believe to have been a vehicle of divine teaching to the nations they addressed, and if so to have been inspired as their possessors believed. The Old Testament, we must remember, before it passed into Christian hands, was exclusively a national book; and our belief in it does not of necessity commit us to any particular theory, for or against the relative inspiration of other national books, however much we may regard them as ultimately destined to fade in its larger light. So far, therefore, from allowing the inspiration of the Old Testament to be discredited, by the fact that other and inferior books made a similar claim, we invert the reasoning, and argue that the claim of the books in question is corroborated by the inspiration of the Old Testament, which rests, as we believe, on such conclusive proof. Nor is there any novelty in such an idea; for it is only a special application of those principles of the Alexandrian school, to which we have already had occasion to refer. 'Perchance,' says St. Clement of Alexandria, 'philosophy was given to the Greeks, directly and primarily, till the Lord should call the Greeks.' And again, 'The barbarian and Greek philosophy has torn off a fragment, not from the mythology of Dionysus, but from the theology of the Eternal Word[1].'

Briefly, to resume: in considering the prehistoric and subhistoric periods of human existence, we came to the conclusion that the picture they

[1] Strom. i. 5 and 13.

presented was nowise inconsistent with a belief, that, behind the hidden scenes of life, God had always been revealing Himself, in however limited a measure, to the minds and hearts and consciences of men. The survey of pre-Christian history confirms the probability of such a belief. For we there find, throughout all races, not merely a tendency to seek after God, but a conviction that God or the gods have revealed and do reveal themselves to men; while in the history and literature of one race the evidence of such a revelation, the intrinsic spiritual evidence, is overwhelmingly strong. It has, of course, been impossible, in so brief a compass, to trace the outlines of this process in any other than an abstract way; but it is one which a detailed study of religious history, with the ample materials now at our command, cannot fail to substantiate in an impartial mind. The human side of religion is, of course, more open to observation than the divine, and hence its history is easily apt to be misrepresented, and misread, as merely the record of a gradual human discovery; but in the eyes of any serious theist, who will be at the pains to think out his creed, this can only be regarded as a subordinate and secondary aspect of a gradual divine revelation. Nor is the gradual nature of the process, as we have seen, any argument against its being divine. Personal intercourse between men, to recur to our previous analogy, is of necessity conditioned, qualified, limited, restrained by their respective capacities for appreciating and comprehending one another. 'No man is a hero to his valet,' not—as Hegel well explains the proverb—because the hero is no hero, but because the valet is only a valet. When we extend this law into the region of our intercourse with God, and consider what qualification such intercourse must demand on the part of man, the facts of history, so far from surprising us, will coincide with what we should expect. Among races whose average morality is low, and spiritual insight dim, few only, very few, will be capable of any inspiration; while these few, in proportion to their fewness, will take long to raise the tone of others; but as the general tone rises and men start from a higher plane, the relative number of religious minds will imperceptibly increase, and react with corresponding power upon their age. While as races differ in their pace of development, in their opportunities and in the use of them, in their capacities and in the drift of them, in their faithfulness to their own best light, the race which first attains the clearest moral and spiritual conceptions will tower aloft by that very fact; as the man of character towers at once over the man of strength, or intellect, or art, and thereby becomes the qualified recipient of a higher degree of revelation. This is in our judgement the course which history has taken; and, moreover, it is the only course which we could antecedently conceive, that the self-revelation of a personal God would be likely to take, since a person can only be revealed, as such, to other persons, in graduated response to their own personal state. And it is immaterial whether we describe this process in terms of human merit or divine election; since merit and election are essentially correlative, two aspects, the obverse and reverse, of one thing.

In the above remarks we have somewhat studiously understated our case, in order to avoid all questions that would inevitably lead off into side issues, and divert attention from the central point. Even so, we cannot, of course, expect an antitheistic opponent to accept at once our interpretation of facts. All that we can do is to point out those facts, as undeniable in their occurrence, unquestionable in their historic importance, suggestive, if not decisive, of their own spiritual interpretation, and in any case demanding to be very seriously weighed. Meanwhile, when we advance our other argumentative reasons for believing in a personal God, we can not admit the superficial but still common rejoinder that history is against us; since history, in our view, makes for us, in no uncertain terms, although, like the other elements of a cumulative argument, it must be read in its complete context to be seen in its true light.

LECTURE VIII

JESUS CHRIST THE DIVINE AND HUMAN PERSON

THE line of thought which we have been pursuing leads us on to the Incarnation[1], as the adequate and final revelation of the personality of God. Of course the Incarnation presupposes that personality, and cannot, therefore, be adduced as an independent argument in its favour. But in the accumulation of probabilities it has nevertheless an important place, as fulfilling the natural anticipation, to which belief in a personal God gives rise, and thus rendering our doctrine harmonious, self-consistent, complete.

Now there can be no question that the most serious objections raised against the Incarnation are really of an *a priori* character. It seems too strange, too paradoxical, too utterly stupendous to be true. Men are staggered as they try to realize it, and half inclined to doubt whether the majority of its professed believers have ever actually thought it out. Thus there is a tendency to approach its

[1] See note 24.

evidence, as contained in the New Testament, with a negative bias, which insensibly necessitates the deduction of negative conclusions. The case is more or less unconsciously prejudged.

But if we ask wherein the intrinsic improbability of the Incarnation consists, we find that it rests upon the open or disguised assumption, that man's rank in nature is determined by the size and situation of his abode in space. We no longer view our planet as the centre of the universe, and our cosmical insignificance is supposed to argue our personal unimportance. It seems inconceivable that amid the limitless immensity of space, and the endless possibilities of time, our earth should have been the scene, and our race the witness, of an unique divine event.

The effect of this line of thought upon the imagination is undoubtedly great, and impairs the faith of many whom it does not explicitly convince. Nevertheless, upon analysis, it may easily be seen to be essentially imaginative, as distinct from rational; and further, it can only be maintained on materialistic grounds, for it makes magnitude, material magnitude, the sole criterion of worth. Whereas, 'If the entire physical universe conspired to crush a man,' as Pascal says, 'the man would still be nobler than the entire physical universe, for he would know that he was crushed [1].' Man, as we

[1] See note 25.

have already seen, knows himself to be spiritual. His thought out-soars space; his love overcomes time; his freedom transcends the laws of merely material existence. He moves in another world than that of sight and sound—a world wherein he feels himself to be still but a beginner; quick with aspirations and faculties and powers, that claim for their due development an illimitable life. The home which he now inhabits may be but one of many mansions that he is ultimately destined to possess.

But if this, which is man's instinctive judgement of himself be true, the attempt to estimate his value by material modes of measurement, or criticize his history by material calculations, is manifestly absurd. If materialism, as we have seen once for all, cannot explain the origin of personality, neither can it forecast or prejudge its destiny, or the events which the course of that destiny may possibly involve. Nor is this all. For in the act of declining to be thus mechanically weighed, our personality lays claim to a loftier method of appreciation; based upon its infelt capacity for intercourse with God, and the consequent conviction that life in that intercourse is its appointed end. The sense of divine nearness, it will have been already noticed, is no invention of Christianity. We have found it in every stage of human development, in every form of human religion. It is rudely conceived by the savage, refinedly by the saint. At times it is a welcome thought, at times overwhelmingly oppressive. But it is persistent enough to be called a characteristic feature of humanity. The gods of Epicurus, lying beside their nectar, are products of abstract reflection, not of unsophisticated instinct. And when all due allowance has been made for the intermittent operation of this mode of thought, it remains historically true that, on the average, man has regarded his gods as near. Sacrifices, tribal communions, systems of taboo, oracles, sacred mysteries with awful rites; the union with Osiris of the Egyptian soul, the avatars of India, the theophanies of Greece, even the blasphemous apotheoses of imperial Rome, are indications of this widespread feeling, which may be separately criticized, but cannot be collectively despised. And in the face of these things it is impossible to say that such an approximation between God and man, as the Incarnation implies, is at all an unnatural thought. If astronomy raises an imaginary presumption against it, psychology bears powerful witness on its behalf, as lying at the very root of the personality of man. The most familiar things seem strange when we pause to make them objects of reflection, from the spelling of a word to the existence of the world. And in this way the Incarnation is surpassingly strange, but not in the sense of contradicting any fundamental necessity of thought. If it be replied that this is only true of the earlier world, and that in fact it does contradict our modern notion of the uniformity of law, we answer, that, waiving the question of the precise value of that notion, the Incarnation is in reality the most consummate exhibition that we can conceive, of God's own obedience to the laws of His creation.

So far, therefore, from admitting any presumption against the Incarnation *a priori*, we contend that the natural human presumption points the other way. For we find the desire for union with God to lie at the very basis of our being, and when once the story of the Incarnation has dawned upon our horizon, we recognize that under the conditions of the world of sin in which we live, nothing else could have so adequately satisfied this inmost aspiration. It must be true we say, because it so incomparably meets our need.

This, however, leads us from *a priori* to evidential considerations; and though we cannot, of course, enter upon Christian evidence in detail, it will be necessary to point out, briefly, its general bearing upon our present inquiry. And in so doing, the first position which it is of importance to maintain is that the Christian religion is one phenomenon, a totality, a whole, of which the New Testament is only a part. We of to-day are in actual contact with a living Christianity, which has persisted through nineteen centuries of human chance and change; and though hindered, now as ever, by schism, treachery, hate, flattery, contempt, presents the same essential features which it presented nineteen centuries ago; miracles of penitence, miracles of purity, miracles of spiritual power; weakness strengthened, fierceness chastened, passion calmed and pride subdued; plain men and philosophers, cottagers and courtiers, living a new life through the faith that Jesus Christ is God. Further, when we have distinguished the Christian spirit from its human corruptions—a distinction which is perfectly legitimate and plain—the verdict of impartial history is unquestionably with us, in asserting that Christianity has justified its claim to be the salt of the earth. For it, and it alone, gave men the ideal and the impulse, which once and for all made progress possible, and parted the modern from the ancient world. Abstract thinkers may say otherwise, but few, who have studied the lives of men, are prepared to deny that Christianity has been the greatest fact in human history.

Yet if this be so it must be obviously impossible to appreciate the New Testament apart from its result — its result in the lives, and deaths, and deeds of Christian men. The New Testament asserts the advent of a fresh power into life; and there are countless Christians now alive who profess experience of that power. The founder of

Christianity is reported to have said, 'Lo, I am with you always, even unto the end of the world.' And serious, sober-minded men may still be found, the whole world over, who say they are conscious of this presence as a fact; while, as a result of this power and presence, the same things are being done and suffered, which were done and suffered in the apostolic and every after-age. The Epistles and Gospels are thus intimately, indissolubly linked with the whole vast movement whose beginning they describe. And any criticism which would radically invalidate their worth, would render the greatest event in history an effect without a cause. Now to construct out of the Gospels an imaginary portrait, of One who neither worked wonders nor claimed to be divine, is to invalidate their worth, for it is to tear them literally into shreds. The conception of Christ, as superhuman, is too completely incorporate in their substance, too subtly inwoven into their tissues, too intimately present in their every line, to be removed by any process short of their destruction as a whole. Moreover, if there were an unknown Christ behind the New Testament, a Christ whom its writers unanimously misrepresented or misunderstood, it would not be on this unknown Person, but on His misrepresentation that Christianity is built. For the absolutely central doctrine round which Christianity has always moved, and which has been the secret of its unique hold upon the hearts and consciences of men, is not simply the loving Fatherhood of God, but the proof that He has given of His loving Fatherhood, by sending His only-begotten Son into the world. Faith in the Incarnation, with all that it involved, has been the sole and exclusive source of our historic Christianity. Yet if Christ were merely man, this was precisely the one point, on which either He or His reporters were profoundly wrong. The case therefore is narrowed to a simple issue. Christianity cannot be due to the goodness and wisdom of a man, marred by a pardonable element of error; for it is simply and solely on the supposed element of error that it rests; and its missionaries, its martyrs, its holy and humble men of heart, all of strongest that human souls have done, all of saintliest that human eyes have seen, will have derived their inspiration either from folly or from fraud.

But if the world is a rational order, as scientific predictions conclusively prove, and a rational order which makes for righteousness, as philosophy and history attest, we cannot attribute the chief episode in its moral development to chance. A cosmos cannot have a chaos for its crown.

Thus we approach the life of Christ, with its deeds of wonder and its words of power—the writings which relate it, themselves a literary marvel —the Jewish expectation which in disappointing it fulfilled—the pagan aspirations which it unexpectedly answered—the secular preparation for its effective appearance—its apposite occurrence—its paradoxical success—and all the various arguments that multiply each other in its behalf, with an antecedent presumption that they must be true. This process is strictly scientific. We have present experience of an unique fact, the Christian life; and we infer an unique cause for its production. The nature of a thing, as Aristotle truly says, is that which it has become, when its process of development is over. And whenever we forget the vital connexion between the present and the past, and study origins without a reference to the things which they originate, our historic method at once degenerates into pedantic antiquarianism. The fact of what man now is proves that his ancestor, however appearing, must really have been more than an ape. The fact of what conscience now feels and does proves that its source, however obscure, was really something other than mere pleasure or utility. And so, the fact of Christian experience is sufficient to convince the Christian, that the founder of his faith was more than man.

We find, then, that Jesus Christ, as depicted in the pages of the New Testament, threw a totally new light upon the personality of man. He took love as His point of departure, the central principle in our nature, which gathers all its other faculties and functions into one; our absolutely fundamental and universal characteristic. He taught us that virtues and graces are only thorough when they flow from love; and further, that love alone can reconcile the opposite phases of our life—action and passion, doing and suffering, energy and pain, since love inevitably leads to sacrifice, and perfect sacrifice is perfect love. It may be granted that previous teachers had said somewhat kindred things. But Jesus Christ carried His precepts home by practice, as none had ever done before. He lived and died the life and death of love; and men saw, as they had never seen, what human nature meant. Here at last was its true ideal, and its true ideal realized. Now the content of man's own personality is, as we have seen, the necessary standard by which he judges all things, human or divine; his final court of critical appeal. Consequently one effect of the life of Christ upon our race was to provide us, if the phrase may be allowed, with a new criterion of God. Man had learned that love was the one thing needful, and had looked into the depths of love, as he had never looked before. And thenceforth love became the only category under which he could be content to think of God.

Religious minds of every race had long been accustomed to conceive of God as possessing in an eminent degree the attributes which they valued most among themselves, and thus as being wiser, mightier, holier than man; and as soon as they saw that love was the true source of all these attributes, men were ready to recognize that God must possess transcendent love. And how could such love be proved except by sacrifice. This thought, however, did not at first arise from abstract reflection; it stole over men's minds unconsciously as they watched and followed Jesus Christ, and was accompanied by the conviction, the slow, gradual, progressive conviction, that Jesus Christ was more than human; was the Son of God; was God, offering Himself in sacrifice for man. (The revelation, and the education of mankind to understand it, were inseparable aspects of the selfsame fact.) *and Revelation, as such, disappears!*

To estimate or criticize the power of the evidence, which first led men to accept this stupendous belief, is in the present, far later, age impossible. Signs and wonders were plainly a part of it, but signs and wonders can only be conclusive to contemporary eyes; the time, the place, the surroundings, the state of the beholder's mind, are a necessary part of this convincing power. And obviously this context cannot now be reconstructed, either in the interests of proof or doubt. For this reason the miracles in question can never be disproved, except by the assumption of *a priori* premisses which

Christians do not grant. While we who believe them, as rooted in our records and congruous with our creeds, still do not rest our faith upon them, or feel serious concern when they are attacked. For, once brought home to the minds of men, the Incarnation is its own evidence. It is there; and how did it come there, and why has it remained there, except by being true? Power was the watchword of its earliest preaching, power over the hearts and consciences of men; and the efforts of nineteen centuries to explain it, to crush it, to corrupt it, have left that mysterious power unimpaired to-day. Even its opponents cannot quietly ignore it, so strangely does it fascinate alike both friend and foe.

We cannot now attempt even to summarize the arguments which converge upon the Incarnation with cumulative force; but we have indicated the framework into which they fit, the map of the region whose details they supply. On the one hand there is the expectation of a personal revelation, historically founded on our religious instincts, and philosophically justified by our analysis of personality. There is the gradual refinement of this expectation till it culminates in the demand for a God of love. And then, at the precise moment when the expectation culminates, and through the same instrumentality by which its final refinement is affected, a revelation purports to come; which, if true, miraculously fits the facts, and in virtue of so doing has moulded history ever since; and which, if in any degree or form untrue, falls hopelessly to pieces, crumbles into fragments, vanishes in air; and yet despite of so doing continues the while to mould mankind, and to mould them for their progress, and their good.

The weight of this dilemma must obviously rest upon the value of man's verdict on himself. Are his religious instincts to be trusted? Are his rational deductions from them true? Are his moral judgements of their issues just? Is he, in fine, that spiritual being, which from ages immemorial he has thought himself to be? We have indicated the reasons for answering this question in the affirmative; nor are they obsolete because they are old. Resting mainly as they do upon introspective analysis, they have been always within reach of philosophic minds; and though perhaps clearer to us than they were to Plato, were yet as convincing to Plato as they are to us. Physical science cannot affect them, for they are essentially metaphysical; but inasmuch as physical science relies upon the validity and veracity of thought, and issues, in virtue of that reliance, in calculations that are daily verified, and predictions that are constantly fulfilled, it bears witness indirectly to all the phenomena of consciousness with which thought is inseparably bound.

But if once we accept what may fairly be called man's natural self-estimate as true, the series of inferences that we have traced begins to follow. His religious instinct points to a Person informing and sustaining material things. His reason and conscience justify this instinct, by demanding a first and final cause and moral governor. He anticipates that this Person will reveal Himself to man, in proportion to man's capacity for receiving His revelation. And when faced by an event which claims to be that revelation, and which, while baffling his every forecast more than fulfils his every hope, he is prepared to accept it as true; and if true, as the final vindication of all his previous processes of thought.

Thus the Incarnation is the crown and climax of all that has gone before; and a Christian cannot possibly separate his creed from the other arguments for a personal God. The validity of those arguments is, of course, unaffected by disbelief in the Incarnation. But they raise, as we have seen, an expectation, which, apart from the Incarnation, is not adequately met; while the Incarnation so completely meets it as to clinch the entire circle of proof.

This, then, is the main outline of our reasons for believing in a personal God; and it suggests two or three reflections. In the first place, these reasons are concrete and not abstract. They rest upon countless and complex facts, which must be known by experience to be judged aright. The moral argument, for example, or the teleological argument, or the value of universal consent, must be realized in imagination before their weight can be felt. And this is a work of patience and of time. Again, these separate arguments unite in one cumulative proof, and what is true of them apart is doubly true of them together : for to appreciate a cumulative argument we must not only realize its elements, but we must further realize the peculiar force of their combination; the way in which each fresh factor makes it harder to reject the rest, till at last they coalesce into one immediate, indissoluble whole. Further, the argument in question is of immense antiquity; and, to feel the strength of its appeal, we must remember the minds that it has satisfied; not merely their number, but their philosophic ability and moral worth; together with the searching controversies, which have modified its statement, while leaving its substantial identity untouched. It is thus no mere chain of reasoning with which we are concerned; it is our whole attitude towards the world; the historic attitude of mankind; a thing which countless currents, from countless sources, through countless ages, have imperceptibly gone to form; brooks flowing into streams, streams swelling into rivers, rivers meeting in oceans, till the earth has become 'full of the knowledge of the Lord as the waters cover the sea.'

But what abstract logic has not created, abstract logic cannot destroy. The ease with which we criticize a picture, or a statue, or a building which we should never have had the genius to construct, may bring home to us the immeasurable distance between abstract and concrete thought. So here, we have before us a theory of the universe; time-honoured, coherent, concrete, positive, august; and abstract criticism is powerless against it. The mere suggestion of a doubt here, and a difficulty there, an uncertainty in this place, or an obscurity in that, is futile, unless supported by some positive hypothesis, to take the place of what it seeks to remove; seeing that, after all, the universe is a fact, and some account of it must needs be true. What, then, are the positive hypotheses which are offered us as substitutes for a personal God? There is Hegel's Idea, as understood—though some of us think misunderstood—by the Hegelians of the left, and misunderstood at the cost of charging their master either with intellectual or moral error. There is the blind Will, which Schopenhauer sought to substitute for the Hegelian Idea. There is the Supra-conscious Unconscious, with which Hartmann sought to improve on Schopenhauer's Will. There is the Moral Order of Fichte, Matthew Arnold's Eternal Not-ourselves, that makes for righteousness.

Now, we have shown above that not one of these notions is conceivable apart from personality. They are derived by abstraction from the various functions of personality, and when severed from their source they become not merely hypothetical, but absolutely meaningless; 'words, mere words; full of sound and fury, signifying nothing.' To say this is not to depreciate the brilliant insight, and suggestive thought, which accompanies the exposition of the theories in question. They are undoubtedly works of genius, but of genius which at times recalls the cynical epigram, that 'metaphysicians are poets run mad.' For, however logically deduced and systematically arranged, they cannot really be called systems, since the central principles, on which they hang, are mere imaginary fictions, unsupported in mid-air; while we feel as we peruse them, that their authors, and adherents alike, have unconsciously personified these cardinal abstractions; and that to this surreptitious re-introduction of personality all their plausibility is really due.

Materialism looks at first sight more solid. But materialism, as we have also seen, is in precisely similar case; since matter regarded by itself is another meaningless abstraction. We only know matter at first hand in our own bodies; there and there alone we are inside it, and can view it from within. But matter in our own bodies is in intimate union with personality. And we have no reason therefore to suppose that matter ever exists or can exist, or that there is such a thing as matter, unsustained by spirit. And what is true of matter is even more obviously true of energy and force.

Thus no positive hypothesis can be offered as a substitute for a personal God, which is not either an abstraction from personality, and therefore demonstrably unreal, or an abstraction inconsistently personified, and therefore demonstrably untrue.

Hence the attraction of Agnosticism, which includes a wide range of opinion, from hypothetical atheism to hypothetical theism; being in fact compatible with any tendency, so long as the tendency in question does not issue in dogmatic belief. The term has been several times defined with an attempt at precision; but its negative nature eludes definition, and it may best therefore be taken in its widest extent. Now the last thing in the world with which Agnosticism desires to be identified is Pyrrhonism, that is the thorough-going scepticism which even doubts that it doubts. On the contrary, it draws a sharp distinction between the known and the unknown, rejecting the latter and accepting the former; as being respectively incapable and capable of proof.

But if there is any truth in the whole course of

P

our previous thought, this distinction is untenable, and the logical Agnostic cannot in the end escape from Pyrrhonism. For Agnosticism professes to rest upon physical science; but physical science makes two assumptions which, after what has been said before, may be very briefly summarized, and which are incompatible with the Agnostic position. In the first place it takes for granted that the universe can be known, or in other words is intelligible. This assumption or conviction is so obvious and universal that it may easily escape notice altogether. But it involves the important conclusion that the universe is a work of mind, since we cannot attribute intelligibility to any source except intelligence. Thus the initial presupposition of physical science is metaphysical, and carries us at once beyond the region which the Agnostic calls 'the known.' Again, physical science assumes that our reasoning faculties are trustworthy. But our reasoning faculties do not stand alone. They are inseparably bound up with our emotions and our will, as part and parcel of our one personality; and the conviction of their veracity must by consequence imply that our other faculties are equally veracious. But our other faculties as inevitably lead us to see moral purpose in the universe, as our reason to see rational arrangement; and here again we are beyond the limits of what the Agnostic 'knows.' To accept these conclusions is to abandon Agnosticism, to reject them is to make any kind of certainty impossible, and reduce all knowledge to mere opinion; in other words to abandon science. In fact to deny divine, is to deny human personality, and this is what the Agnostic really does. He ignores or explains away the elements in man which point to God; and thus while professing to trust experience invalidates its very source, by discrediting the primary instincts, and natural operations of the mind through which experience comes[1].

There remains the hypothesis of a personal God, a Being whose mode of existence is indeed beyond our power to conceive; but who, in however transcendent a manner, thinks, wills, loves, and holds personal intercourse with persons. If our human personality were a fixed and finite thing, it would supply us with no analogue for conceiving such a Being; but we have seen that it is not a fixed and finite thing, but a seed, a germ, a potency, a 'herald of itself in higher place.' We can imagine it existing, almost infinitely magnified, in capacity and character, in intensity and scope; and we have a presage that such existence is its destined goal. Thus while all else around us is rigorously finite, personality alone suggests infinitude of life; and however much, when applied to

[1] See note 26.

God, it out-soars the field of our vision, we feel that in using the term we are using words that have a meaning. We are thinking, not refusing to think; in other words, that a Personal God is a positive conception. Further, we have seen that personality is triune, and is met by the revelation of a triune God. Of the first point there can be no question. The relation of a subject to an object is absolutely fundamental to the notion of a person, and thus lands us in triunity at once. The only question that can plausibly be raised is, not whether human personality is triune, but whether that triunity gave rise to our triune conception of God; so that the latter is in fact an invention, not a revelation. The answer to this is that beyond question we can trace the process by which the doctrine of the Trinity took theological form. It started in the concrete, with the baptismal formula of the Christian Church, a practical provision for a practical need, emanating from Jesus Christ. And throughout the history of its dogmatic formulation, we are confronted with this fact. It was regarded as a revelation by the men who shaped its intellectual expression; and it was only in the process, the very gradual process of that expression, that its congruity with human psychology came out; that psychology in fact being distinctly developed in the effort to give it utterance. No one contributed more to this philosophical work than St. Augustine; yet the words of the prayer with which he concludes his treatise on the Trinity show plainly what he believed to be its source.

'O Lord our God, we believe in Thee, the Father and the Son and the Holy Ghost. For the truth would not say, Go, baptize all nations in the name of the Father and of the Son and of the Holy Spirit, unless Thou wast a Trinity. Nor wouldest Thou, O Lord God, bid us be baptized in the name of Him who is not the Lord God[1].'

The same is the case with Origen, Athanasius, Hilary, Basil, and the Gregories. They did not accommodate Christian religion to their philosophy, but philosophy to their Christian religion. Thus we are met by what claims to be the self-revelation of the Personal God. It appeals first to elemental humanity in the hearts of unsophisticated men; far removed from Alexandria or Athens; yet the very words in which it does so, turn out, upon analysis, to involve a view of personality which the world had not attained, but which, once stated, is seen to be profoundly, philosophically true. But if a view of God which is so consonant with philosophical analysis, as often to have been mistaken for a product of philosophy, can be shown to have entered the world, among the fishermen of Galilee, in wholly unphilosophical disguise, its

[1] *De Trin.*

claim to revelation is immensely strengthened by the fact. Moreover there was a sufficient reason for such a revelation. For the truth which is revealed was what made the Incarnation possible, and gave entirely new meaning to the thought that God is Love. Since love is of two kinds: the love of inferiors, and the love of equals; the love of condescension, and the love of mutual affection. And however much in pre-Christian ages men had thought of the love of God, they could not regard it otherwise than as the love of condescension; of the infinitely greater for the infinitely less; in technical terms, an accident contingent on creation; not the essence of God Himself. But a God, within whose Being are personal distinctions, can at once be conceived as essentially, eternally, absolutely Love; love of which the human analogue is passion and not pity; the intensest, mightiest, holiest thing we know.

And this new insight into the divine nature, threw a new light upon the destiny of man, as capable, through the Incarnation, of being made holy in the Beloved, and so raised from the level of pity to be partaker of the eternal love of God. Thus the actual Trinity of God explains the potential trinity of man; and our anthropomorphic language follows from our theomorphic minds [1].

These considerations bring us round again to

---

[1] See note 27.

the point from which we started, and from which we will briefly resume.

Human personality has attributes, self-consciousness and freedom, which distinguish it in kind from the world of mere animals and things, and relate it to a spiritual order, of whose eminent reality it is itself at once the witness and the proof. With this conviction in his mind, man looks at the universe outside him, and divines there, with an instinct which age or argument cannot eradicate, the presence of a Person, whom he feels, but may not see. On reflection this grows more certain; for the world is rational, harmonious, beautiful; it works out moral purposes; and must therefore have a spiritual cause; and these are notes of personality, and of personality alone. When he asks why, if this be so, God has not made Himself more manifest, he is met by the analogy of human intercourse, and the restriction which sin imposes, even on the knowledge of a saintly friend. This qualifies the views with which he enters upon history; and history presents the picture that he is led to expect; ignorant ages dimly aware of deity around them; national progress answered by national enlightenment; increase of personal insight met by increase of inspiration; the race that is eminent in desire of holiness selected for eminence in degree of revelation. At length, as is meet, from the holy race, comes forth the Holy One; guiding man into the life of love, wherein his true perfection lies; and revealing God as the source of love, and Himself as God incarnate; in union with Whom our finite, imperfect personality, shall find, in the far eternity, its archetype and end.

NOTES

LECTURE I

NOTE 1. Page 3.

Things new and old. 'To us the history of philosophy has become a part of philosophy itself, because we have learned to look on the speculations of earlier times, not as dogmatic systems to be accepted or rejected, but rather as the first stages in the progressive evolution of a thought of which, in a further stage, we ourselves are the organs and interpreters. Hence follow two important consequences. On the one hand, we are freed to some extent from historical partisanship, since we do not expect to find direct support for our own ideas in any past system; yet, on the other hand, we are enabled to feel a living interest in all such systems, as containing aspects or elements of the truth which we seek to discover. We are pledged to show that the system which we regard as true is the result of a synthesis in which those aspects or elements are combined.' (E. Caird, *Phil. of Kant*, i. 68.)

This general attitude of mind, which our modern

historic method has produced, is as important in theology as in philosophy. There, too, we are at once the children and the critics of the past,—the past which is never obsolete, or of merely antiquarian interest, but a necessary element in the life and knowledge of to-day. In the present case, both the antiquity and the adaptability of the arguments for a personal God must be borne in mind. The arguments in question are so fundamental as to have commended themselves to man, as soon as he began seriously to reflect upon religion; and at the same time so inexhaustible as to admit of continual adaptation, to the ideas and idiosyncrasies of every successive age. They thus combine the authority of age with the versatility of youth; and the fact of this combination multiplies their force. If the patristic and scholastic passages, in the following notes, are compared with those from later writers, it will be noticed that they indicate a substantial identity of doctrine; remaining unaltered in its essence, though continuously modified in form.

'L'esprit humain, sans doute, va s'étendre à des objets nouveaux, et briller avec plus d'éclat dans quelques-uns de ses rayons; mais il ne changera pas ses lois. Il approfondira ses acquisitions antérieures; il complétera, vérifiera ce qu'il avait déjà trouvé, et, selon une admirable expression de la Sainte Écriture, *il renouvellera la sagesse ;* mais nous verrons que la lumière n'a pas changé, et que la sagesse renouvelée est, en effet, toujours ancienne et toujours nouvelle.' (Gratry, *Con. de Dieu,* i. 356.)

NOTE 2. Page 25.

Science and Theology equally anthropomorphic. 'There are but three forms under which it is possible to think of the ultimate or immanent principle of the Universe,—Mind, Life, Matter: given the first, it is intellectually thought out: the second, it blindly grows: the third, it mechanically shuffles into equilibrium. From what school do we draw these types of conception? from our home experiences? if it is because we are rational, that we see reason around us, no less is it because we are alive, that we believe in the living, and because we have to deal with our own weight and extension, that we make acquaintance with material things. Take away these properties of the ego, and should we ever find what they are in the non-ego? Assuredly not. Man is equally your point of departure, whether you discern in the cosmos an intellectual, a physiological, or a mechanical system: and the only question is whether you construe it by his highest characteristics, or by the middle attributes which he shares with other organisms; or by the lowest, that are absent from no physical things. . . . In every doctrine, therefore, it is still from our microcosm that we have to interpret the macrocosm: and from the type of our humanity, as presented in self-knowledge, there is no more escape for the pantheist or the materialist, than for the theist. Modify them as you may, all causal conceptions are born from within, as reflections or reductions of our personal, animal, or physical activity: and the severest science is, in this sense, just as anthropomorphic as the most ideal theology.' (Martineau, *A Study of Religion,* i. 336.)

'That knowledge, or what passes for knowledge, soon gets ... beyond the data of perception and the powers of imagination, is a fact which comes to the surface more prominently in Theology perhaps than in Science. I am not aware that this is because there is any essential philosophic difference between these two great departments of knowledge. It arises rather from the fact that, for controversial purposes, it has been found convenient to dwell on the circumstance that our idea of the Deity is to a certain extent necessarily anthropomorphic, while the no less certain, if somewhat less obvious, truth that our idea of the external world is also anthropomorphic, does not supply any ready argumentative weapon.... The world as represented to us by Science can no more be perceived or imagined than the Deity as represented to us by Theology, and ... in the first case, as in the second, we must content ourselves with symbolical images, of which the thing we can most certainly say is that they are not only inadequate, but incorrect.' (A. Balfour, *Defence of Philosophic Doubt*, xii. 244.)

'We recognize ... psychological anthropomorphism, from the Ideas of Plato, to the immanent dialectic of the cosmical process of Hegel, and to the unconscious Will of Schopenhauer.' (Helmholtz, *Thought in Medicine*, Popular Scientific lectures, vol. ii.)

'By the necessity of language it would seem that any definition of the conception of God must, so far as it is not pure negation, suggest either a being human in respect of the highest attributes of humanity, or else some being inferior to humanity. Take, for example, the well-known definition (how skilfully and gracefully advocated every one knows) that God is "the Eternal, not ourselves, that makes for righteousness." Now, what is meant here by the word *makes*? For the word necessarily calls up three, and only three, kinds of "making"; either "making" voluntarily, as a man makes; or "making" instinctively, as a beast makes; or "making" neither voluntarily nor instinctively, but unconsciously, just as an eddy or current may be said to "make." Of these three kinds of "making," which is meant? If the first, you are anthropomorphic; if the second, you are zoomorphic; if the third, you are azoomorphic. Supposing each of these three hypotheses to be dangerous, I should prefer the first as the least dangerous. But if you say that you prefer not to define what sort of "making" you mean, and that you will leave this an open question, then I should reply that such a use of words rather conceals than reveals thought, and conveys (as perhaps indeed it is intended to convey) no revelation whatever of the nature of God.' (Abbot, *Through Nature to Christ*, i. 44.)

'... Those who, out of a conscientious regard for the interests of Science, have felt themselves compelled to derive Organic Life from blind chance, and purposeless matter ... have invested their original principles with so much reason and power of internal development, that nothing but the caprice of their terminology which keeps to the names of Matter, Mechanism, and Accident, for what other people call Spirit, Life, and Providence, seems to prevent them from relapsing into notions which they had before strenuously opposed.' (Lotze, *Metaphysic*, § 236, E. T.)

'Surely it is too plain for words that *all* our thought and all our feeling *must be* anthropomorphic. The proposal to avoid anthropomorphism is as absurd as the suggestion that we should take an unbiassed outside view of ourselves by jumping out of our skin.' (*Riddles of the Sphinx*, by a Troglodyte, p. 145.)

LECTURE II

NOTE 3. Page 28.

The introspective method. 'Internal observation has for its matter intuition and the objects intuited, the feelings, the perceptions, and all that a man perceives within himself. Hence internal observation is the source of the initial sciences of philosophy, Ideology and Psychology. External observation is the starting-point of all the physical sciences. To the faithful, practical application of this principle must be ascribed the wonderful progress made by the physical and mechanical sciences in modern times; and it is to the neglect of internal observation that is due the backward condition of those sciences which rest on it. The strangest feature in the case is, that these sciences were even dwarfed and loaded with most superficial prejudices by those very persons who with most ostentation proclaimed the method of observation and experience. The reason was that they prized *external observation*, but did not know *internal observation*. They preached and lauded observation in general, at the same time ignoring that species of observation which would have been most useful to them. Directing their attention only to external observation, which is valid only for material things, and not for mind (*spirito*), they arrived at two unfortunate results: (1) They sterilized the metaphysical sciences by rejecting certain things not supplied by external experience; (2) They materialized and wasted these sciences, transferring to the sphere of spiritual things what was derived from external observation, and could belong only to material things.' (Rosmini, *Logic*, § 951, qu. by T. Davidson.)

'As we recede further back, we pass more and more into the dark: of our childhood, a few broken gleams from vivid moments yet remain: of our infancy all trace is gone; and of that human period we can affirm nothing psychological, except by inference or conjecture from observations newly made on others. As this is a much more precarious source of knowledge, we are warranted in saying that our confidence in it should be graduated accordingly; and that our imaginary constructions drawn from it should be severely tested by the immediate contents of our existing or unforgotten self-consciousness. Instead of this superior deference to our most assured inner experience, I find a disposition ... to take liberties with the testimony of our present thought and feeling, and put it out of court, or give it a colouring not its own, on the ground that it has grown old and is no longer what it was, and that it is of very little use appealing to so altered a state of psychological facts..... The empirical analysis assumes *an amount* of alteration in our ideas from first to last, and takes the benefit of it, which I believe to be wholly unwarranted; and, in trusting the form which they present in our matured intelligence, we are less likely to be deceived, than in reverting to the crude type of even their rightly construed germs.' (Martineau, *A Study of Religion*, ii. 213.)

NOTE 4. Page 28.

Self-consciousness. Self-consciousness may be called the form of personality. It is that which converts animal appetites into human desires (see note 5) and which alone makes freedom possible (see note 6); while its self-diremption, its combination of unity with plurality, of identity with difference, separates it, *toto caelo*, from the material order, and therefore from the jurisdiction of the sciences which deal with that order, and constitutes it a spiritual thing. The introspective Augustine developed the significance of self-consciousness more fully than any of his predecessors in the Western world; while the schoolmen did little more than clothe his thoughts upon the subject, in more accurate and appropriate phraseology.

'Quo pacto se aliquid scientem scit, quae se ipsam nescit? neque enim alteram mentem scientem scit, sed se ipsam. Scit igitur se ipsam, etc. etc.' (Aug. *De Trin.* x. 3.)

The following scholastic passages are quoted by Kleutgen.

'Anima rationalis secundum actum proprium nata est super se reflecti cognoscendo se et amando.' (St. Bonav. *In lib. ii.* dist. xix. a. 1. q. 1.)

'Intellectus intelligit se; quod non contingit in aliqua virtute, cujus operatio fit per organum corporale.' (Id. *Ib.*)

'Nullus sensus se ipsum cognoscit nec suam operationem: visus enim non videt seipsum nec videt se videre; sed hoc superioris potentiae est. Intellectus

autem cognoscit seipsum, et cognoscit se intelligere.'
(St. Thom. *Contr. Gent.* lib. ii. c. 66. n. 4.)

> 'Un' alma sola,
> Che vive e sente e sè in sè rigira.'
>
> (Dante, *Purg.* 25, 73.)

'The Ego is not a mere fact, which exists as the Dogmatist conceives a "thing" to exist; it is existence and knowledge of existence in one. Intelligence not only is; it looks on at its own existence. It is *for itself,* whereas the very notion of a thing is that it does not exist for itself, but only for another—that is for some intelligence.' (Seth, *Hegelianism and Personality,* p. 43.)

'In all consciousness of self we know ourselves as persons; in all knowledge of other objects we know them as different from ourselves, and ourselves as different from them. Every man is convinced of this; no man can be made to think otherwise. If there be a God, then, as all His works proclaim, He must be different from at least one part of His works, He must be different from me. In the construction of his artificial system of *a priori* forms, Kant most unfortunately omitted the knowledge of a personal self, and thus speculation, in the hands of his successors, was allowed to flow out into a dreary waste of pantheism. When we restore the conviction of the separate existence of self, and the belief in our continued personality to its proper place, we are rearing an effective barrier in the way of the possible introduction of any system in which man can be identified with God or with anything else.' (McCosh, *Intuitions of Mind,* p. 453.)

'Is He not all but thou, that hast power to feel "I am I."' (Tennyson, *Higher Pantheism.*)

NOTE 5. Page 29.

Desire. 'Appetitus est inclinatio *cognoscentis in cognitum.*' (St. Thom. Aq. *Sum.* i. 80. 1.)

'Desire is feeling accompanied with the additional sense of self-hood—the self extends ideally beyond its limit. The self should be a synthesis of its real organism and its environment, and desire expresses this.' (W. T. Harris, *Hegel's Logic*, p. 393.)

'Self-consciousness seems ... to take into itself the content of a sensitive individuality without making it other than it was as such content. But it is obvious, from the transcendental point of view, that this conception, according to which the consciousness of self is simply filled with a content which it leaves unchanged and to which it adds nothing, is inadequate and misleading. A conscious subject cannot take into itself any particular content which it does not distinguish from itself as such subject, and which again it does not connect with all the other content present to it in its objects. Thus, the self as subject, in being conscious of the desires that belong to its individual sensibility as desires that determine it as one object among others, necessarily separates itself from those desires and from itself as such an object. In other words, while it determines itself as one object among others it by that very fact ceases *to be* simply one object among others. In the consciousness of my desires as particular impulses which determine me as an object in relation to other objects, there is, therefore, a separation of my will from such desires; and as a consequence, a necessity for distinguishing between the simple feeling of pleasure, which comes of the satisfaction of such desires, and the consciousness that *I* am satisfied. In this way, transcendental reflexion forces us to recognize that the conscious self as such is not in immediate identity with the natural impulses; and therefore that its yielding itself to them is always an act of self-determination.' (E. Caird, *Critical Phil. of Kant*, ii. 199.)

'In the consciousness of desire the self is withdrawn from immediate union with the desire; it has the desire before it as a motive, which stands in relation to all other motives through its relation to the self.' (Id. *ib.* p. 217.)

'So soon as any desire has become more than an indefinite yearning for we know not what, so soon as it is really desire *for some object of which we are conscious*, it necessarily involves an employment of the understanding upon those conditions of the real world which make the difference, so to speak, between the object as desired and its realization. . . . It is only the fallacy of taking the pleasure that ensues on satisfaction of a desire to be the object of the desire, which blinds us to this.' (T. H. Green, *Proleg. to Ethics*, §§ 134-5.)

NOTE 6. Page 29.

The freedom of the will is the very nerve of personality; and the variety of the terminology used by its different advocates, in different ages, must not be allowed to obscure the great philosophic tradition in which they agree. It is a case, indeed, in which the appeal to 'the authority of philosophy' is of especial use. For the freedom of the will is really attacked on *a priori* grounds, and defended on grounds of experience; i.e. it is attacked as being inconsistent with various natural analogies, or theoretic presumptions, and defended as being a fact of which we are directly and immediately aware. Now many a man, when he finds acute thinkers discrediting a primary verdict of his consciousness, is apt, with superfluous humility, to think they must be more clever than they seem, and therefore to defer to their authority. It is important, therefore, to draw attention to the fact that the immense weight of philosophic authority is beyond question on the other side. Schopenhauer, the ablest of modern determinists, has also appealed to his predecessors in his own support; and a glance at his list alone should suffice to justify the above statement. Among the not very numerous names occur Jeremiah, Shakespeare, and Sir Walter Scott.

'All the Greek Fathers, as well as the apologists Justin, Tatian, Athenagoras, Theophilus, and the Latin author Minucius Felix, also the theologians of the Alexandrian school, Clement and Origen, exalt the αὐτεξούσιον (the autonomy, self-determination) of the human soul with the freshness of youth and a tincture of Hellenistic idealism, but also influenced by a practical Christian interest. . . . Even Irenaeus, although opposed to speculation, and the more austere Tertullian, strongly insist upon this self-determination in the use of the freedom of the will, from the practical and moral point of view.' (Hagenbach, *Hist. of Doctrines*, § 57.)

'᾿Ελεύθερον καὶ αὐτεξούσιον ἐποίησεν ὁ θεὸς ἄνθρωπον.' (Ath. *ad Autol.* ii. 27.)

'Liberum et sui arbitrii et suae potestatis invenio hominem a Deo institutum.' (Tert. *ad Marc.* ii. 5.)
'Definimus animam ... liberam arbitrii.' (Id. *De An.* 22.)
'Homo rationabilis et secundum hoc similis Deo,

liber in arbitrio factus, et suae potestatis ipse sibi causa est.' (Irenaeus, iv. 4. 231.)

'Voluntas nostra nec voluntas esset, nisi esset in nostra potestate. Porro quia est in potestate, libera est nobis.' (Aug. *De lib. arb.* iii. 8.)

' Noli mirari, si caeteris per liberam voluntatem utimur, etiam ipsa libera voluntate per eam ipsam uti nos posse, ut quodam modo se ipsa utatur voluntas quae utitur caeteris, sicut se ipsam cognoscit ratio, quae cognoscit et caetera.' (Id. *ib.* ii. 51.)

'Arbitrium idem est, quod judicium, ad cujus nutum ceterae virtutes moventur et obediunt. Judicare autem illius est, secundum rationem completam, cujus est discernere inter justum et injustum, et inter proprium et alienum : nulla autem potentia novit, quid justum et quid injustum, nisi illa sola, quae est particeps rationis et nata est cognoscere summam justitiam, a qua est regula omnis juris: hoc autem solum est in ea substantia, quae est ad imaginem Dei, qualis est tantum substantia rationalis. *Nulla enim substantia discernit, quid proprium et quid alienum, nisi cognoscat seipsam et actum suum proprium : sed nunquam aliqua potentia seipsam cognoscit vel supra seipsam reflectitur, quae sit alligata materiae.* Si igitur omnes potentiae sunt alligatae materiae et substantiae corporali praeter solam rationalem, sola illa est, quae potest se super seipsam reflectere ; et ideo ipsa sola est, in qua est plenum judicium et arbitrium in discernendo.' (St. Bonav. *In lib. ii.* dist. xxv. p. 111, qu. by Kleutgen.)

'Nihil in homine sublimius, nihil dignius libero arbitrio ... in quo ad imaginem Dei creatus est. *Principatur omnibus liberi arbitrii ultroneus consensus.*' (R. de St. Victor, *De Stat. Int. Hom.* i. 3. 6.)

'Natura rationalis, quae est Deo vicinissima, non solum habet inclinationem in aliquid sicut habent inanimata, nec solum movens hanc inclinationem quasi aliunde ei determinatam sicut natura sensibilis; sed ultra hoc *habet in potestate ipsam inclinationem*, ut non sit ei necessarium inclinari ad appetibile apprehensum, sed possit inclinari vel non inclinari; et sic ipsa inclinatio non determinatur ei ab alio, sed a se ipsa.' (St. Thom. Aq. *De Verit.*, q. 22, a. 4.)

'Ista est generalis differentia hominis ex una parte, et omnium aliarum rerum et operationum illarum ex parte altera, quia homo, in quantum homo operatur ex libero arbitrio, sed aliae res operantur ex necessitate.' (Raymond de Sabunde, *Theol. Nat.* 82.)

'La substance libre se détermine par elle-même et cela suivant le motif du bien aperçu par l'entendement qui l'incline sans la nécessiter.' (Leibniz, *Théodicée*, § 288.)

Cf. Shakespeare—

'A free determination
'Twixt right and wrong.'

(*Troilus and Cressida*, ii. 3.)

'In every act of will there is an essential freedom, of which the mind is conscious. The possession of a free will is thus one of the elements which go to constitute man a moral and responsible agent ... This truth is revealed to us by immediate consciousness, and is not to be set aside by any other truth whatever. It is a first truth equal to the highest, to no one of which will it ever yield. It cannot be set aside by any other truth whatever, nor even by any other first truth, and certainly by no derived truth. Whatever other proposition is true, this is true also, that man's will is free.' (McCosh, *Intuitions of Mind*, iv. 308.)

'I have a real power of *resisting* my will's stable spontaneous impulse. I am not its *slave*; though neither am I in such sense its *master* that I can at once compel it to desist from its urgent solicitations. I can exercise "self-government" and "self-restraint." While my will's spontaneous impulse remains both stable and powerful, I can, nevertheless, refuse to do what it prompts. I see plainly the very serious evils which will befall me, if I blindly follow its solicitation. And I feel that I can act in a way which is on the one hand accordant with *reason*, while on the other hand it is opposed to *desire* and *impulse*. However vehemently impulse may press me to the unreasonable course, at that very moment, in the teeth of that very impulse, I can exercise what we call "anti-impulsive effort."' (W. G. Ward, *Philosophy of Theism*, ii. 7.)

'Though we now most commonly apply the term "will" to the direction of the conscious self to action, as opposed to a mere wish not amounting to such direction, yet the usage has been by no means uniform. ... But though we cannot fix the usage of words, it is clear that the important real distinction is that between the direction of the self-conscious self to the realization of an object, its identification of itself with that object, on the one side, ... and, on the other side, the mere solicitations of which a man is conscious, but with none of which he so identifies himself as to make the soliciting object his object—the object of his self-seeking—or to direct himself to its realization. ... These other "desires" ... are influences or tendencies by which the man, the self, is affected, not a motion proceeding from him. They tend to move him, but *he* does not move in them; and none of them actually moves him unless the man takes it into himself, identifies himself with it, in a way which wholly alters it from what it was as a mere influence affecting him.' (T. H. Green, *Proleg. to Ethics*, §§ 143-4.)

'Far from admitting that the play of our motives constitutes a necessity and carries off our personality, we are well aware that they are subject to our estimate, and that we choose for ourselves. We are not the theatre, and they the agents; we are the agents, and they, the data of the problems which we solve.' (Martineau, *Study of Religion*, i. 248.)

'No one can sincerely deem himself incapable by nature of controlling his impulses and modifying his acquired character. That he is able to make them the objects of examination, comparison, and estimate, places him in a judicial and authoritative attitude towards them, and would have no meaning if he were not to decide what influence they should have. The casting vote and verdict upon the offered motives is with him, and not with themselves; he is "free" to say "Yes" or "No" to any of their suggestions: they are the conditions of the act; he is its agent.' (Id. *l. c.* ii. 229.)

Cf. *Riddles of the Sphinx* (Appendix), where the fallacy of deriving will from causation, instead of causation from will is well pointed out; e. g. 'The will is the original and more definite archetype, of which causation is a derivative, vaguer and fainter ectype.... So far from being an exception to the universal law of causation, the freedom of the will is the only case in which causation denotes a real fact and is more than a theory.' (*R. of S.*, p. 462.)

Cf. Maine de Biran, 'L'idée de cause a son type primitif et unique dans le sentiment du moi, identifié avec celui de l'effort.' (*Œuvres Inédites*, i. 288.) See also Chandler, *The Spirit of Man*, chap. iv.

NOTE 7. Page 38.

Unity of the ego or self. 'Definimus animam dei flatu natam, immortalem, corporalem, effigiatam, *substantia simplicem*, de suo sapientem, varie procedentem, liberam arbitrii, accedentiis obnoxiam, per ingenia mutabilem, rationalem, dominatricem, divinatricem, ex una redundantem.' (Tertullian, *De Anima*, xxii.)

'Hoc modo anima definiri potest juxta suae proprietatem naturae: anima seu animus est spiritus intellectualis, rationalis, semper in motu, semper vivens, bonae malaeque voluntatis capax. . . . Atque secundum officium operis sui variis nuncupatur nominibus: anima est, dum vivificat; dum contemplatur spiritus est; dum sensit sensus est; dum sapit animus est; dum intelligit mens est; dum discernit ratio est; dum consentit voluntas est; dum recordatur memoria est. Non tamen haec ita dividentur in substantia, sicut in nominibus; quia haec omnia una est anima.' (Alcuin, *De An. Rat.* 149.)

'Le moi est la seule unité qui nous soit donnée immédiatement par la nature; nous ne la rencontrons dans aucune des choses que nos facultés observent. Mais l'entendement qui la trouve en lui, la met hors de lui par induction, et d'un certain nombre de choses coexistantes il crée des unités artificielles.' (M. Royer Collard, qu. in Jouffroy's *Reid*, iv. 350.)

'The union of individuality and universality in a single manifestation, with the implication that the individuality is the essential and permanent element to which the universality is almost in the nature of an accident, is what forms the cardinal point in Personality.' (Wallace, *Proleg. to Hegel*, c. xviii. p. 234)

'A knowledge of sequent states is only possible when each is accompanied by the "I think" of an identical apperception. Or, as it has been otherwise expressed, there is all the difference in the world between succession and consciousness of succession, between change and consciousness of change. Mere change, or mere succession, if such a thing were possible, would be, as Kant points out, first A, then B, then C, each filling out existence for the time being and constituting its sum, then vanishing tracelessly to give place to its successor—to a successor which yet would not be a successor, seeing that no record of its predecessor would remain. The change, the succession, the series can only be known to a consciousness or subject which is not identical with any one member of the series, but is present equally to every member, and identical with itself throughout. Connexion or relatedness of any sort—even Hume's association—is possible only through the presence of such a unity to each term of the relation. Hence, while it is quite true, as Hume said, that when we enter into what we call ourselves, we cannot point to any particular perception of self, as we can point to particular perceptions of heat or cold, love or hatred, it is as undoubted that the very condition of all these particular perceptions, given along with each of them and essential to the connecting of one with another, is precisely the self or subject which Hume could not find—which he could not find because he looked for it not in its proper character, as the subject or correlate of all perceptions or objects, but as itself, in some fashion, a perception or object added to the other contents of consciousness.' (Seth, *Hegelianism and Personality*, i. p. 11.)

'It has been required of any theory which starts without presuppositions and from the basis of experience, that in the beginning it should speak only of sensations or ideas, without mentioning the soul to which, it is said, we hasten without justification to ascribe them. I should maintain, on the contrary, that such a mode of setting out involves a wilful departure from that which is actually given in experience. A mere sensation without a subject is nowhere to be met with as a fact.... It is thus, and thus only, that the sensation is a given fact; and we have no right to abstract from its relation to its subject because this relation is puzzling, and because we wish to obtain a starting-point which looks more convenient but is utterly unwarranted by experience. In saying this I do not intend to repeat the frequent but exaggerated assertion, that in every single act of feeling or thinking there is an express consciousness which regards the sensation or idea simply as states of a self; on the contrary, every one is familiar with that absorption in the content of a sensuous perception which often makes us entirely forget our personality in view of it. But then the very fact that we can become aware that this *was* the case, presupposes that we afterwards retrieve what we omitted at first, viz. the recognition that the perception was in us as our state. Further ... any comparison of two ideas, which ends by our finding their contents like or unlike, presupposes the absolutely indivisible unity of that which compares them.... And so our whole inner world of thoughts is built up; not as a mere collection of manifold ideas, existing with or after one another, but as a world in which these individual members are held together and arranged by the relating activity of this single pervading principle. This then is what we mean by the unity of consciousness; and it is this that we regard as the sufficient ground for assuming an indivisible soul.' (Lotze, *Metaphysic*, bk. iii. c. i. § 241.)

For some remarks on the criticism of the 'Self' contained in Bradley, *Appearance and Reality*, see J. S. Mackenzie, *Mind*, New Series, No. xi.

NOTE 8. Page 43.

Personality the ultimate reality. 'There is nothing else except itself, by which we can understand or explain personality.... The word suggests, not so much the presence of intelligence, will, &c., but more eminently the fact of being a centre to which the universe of being appears in relation, a distinct centre of being, a subject, whereof reason, affection, will, consciousness itself, are so many—(not separate parts, but)—several aspects or activities.... Consciousness is not the ultimate fact in man except when it is tacitly taken as equivalent to self-consciousness, the realization of his own personality. Not the fact that he thinks, but the fact that he is that of which thought-capacity is an aspect or corollary, is the primary datum of all knowledge and thought. He thinks, indeed, likes, wills, acts; but that central fact of which these all are but so many partial aspects is the fact that he is a self.... Personality, involving, as necessary qualities of its being, reason, will, love, is incomparably the highest phenomenon known to experience, and as such has to be related with whatever is above it and below it by any philosophy based on experience.' (R. C. Moberly, *Church Congress*, 1891.)

'This self-personality, like all other simple and immediate presentations, is indefinable; but it is so, because it is superior to definition. It can be analyzed into no simpler elements, for it is itself the simplest of all; it can be made no clearer by description or comparison, for it is revealed to us in all the clearness of an original intuition, of which description and comparison can furnish only faint and partial resemblances.' (Mansel, *Prolegomena Logica*.)

'The cogito of Descartes is not designed to express the phenomena of reflection alone, but is co-extensive with the entire consciousness. This is expressly affirmed in the *Principia*, p. 1, § 9. "Cogitationis nomine intelligo illa omnia, quae nobis consciis in nobis fiunt, quatenus eorum in nobis conscientia est. Atque ita non modo intelligere, velle, imaginari, sed etiam sentire, idem est hic quod cogitare." The dictum, thus extended, may perhaps be advantageously modified by disengaging the essential from the accidental features of consciousness; but its main principle remains unshaken; namely, that our conception of real existence, as distinguished from appearance, is derived from, and depends upon, the distinction between the one conscious subject and the several objects of which he is conscious. The rejection of consciousness, as the primary constituent of substantive existence, constitutes Spinoza's point of departure from the principles of Descartes, and at the same time, the fundamental error of his system.' (Mansel, *Bampt. Lect.* 3, note 25.)

'When Descartes took his *cogito ergo sum* as alone certain, and provisionally regarded the existence of the world as problematical, he really discovered the essential and only right starting-point of all philosophy, and at the same time its *true* foundation. This foundation is essentially and inevitably the *subjective*, the *individual consciousness*. For this alone is and remains immediate; everything else, whatever it may be, is mediated and conditioned through it, and is therefore dependent upon it.' (Schopenhauer, *World as Will and Idea*, bk. i. chap. i, E. T.)

See also Momerie, *Personality the Beginning and End of Metaphysics*.

NOTE 9. Page 48.

Matter an abstraction, and therefore Materialism an absurdity. 'The fundamental absurdity of materialism is that it starts from the *objective*, and takes as the ultimate ground of explanation something *objective*, whether it be matter in the abstract, simply as it is *thought*, or after it has taken form, is empirically given—that is to say is *substance*, the chemical element with its primary relations. Some such thing it takes, as existing absolutely and in itself, in order that it may evolve organic nature and finally the knowing subject from it, and explain them adequately by means of it; whereas in truth all that is objective is already determined as such in manifold ways by the knowing subject through its forms of knowing, and presupposes them; and consequently it entirely disappears if we think the subject away. Thus materialism is the attempt to explain what is immediately given us by what is given us indirectly.' (Schopenhauer, *World as Will and Idea*, bk. i. chap. vii, E. T.)

'Realism (materialism) which commends itself to the crude understanding, by the appearance which it assumes of being matter-of-fact, really starts from an arbitrary assumption, and is, therefore, an empty castle in the air, for it ignores or denies the first of all facts, that all that we know lies within consciousness. For that the *objective existence* of things is conditional through a subject whose ideas they are, and consequently that the objective world exists only as *idea*, is no hypothesis, and still less a dogma, or even a paradox set up for the sake of discussion; but it is the most certain and the simplest truth.' (Schopenhauer, *World as Will and Idea*, bk. i. sup. chap. i, E. T.)

'Let it not be supposed that matter *per se*, can be reached *by the way of inference*. Whatever can be conceived inferentially, must be conceived as the object of *possible*, though not of actual cognition. But there is no potential knowledge, in any quarter, of matter *per se*. . . . It can be conceived only as the object of no possible knowledge; and therefore it cannot be conceived as an inference, except on the understanding that this inference is a finding of the contradictory, or of that which cannot be conceived on any terms by any intelligence.' (Ferrier's *Institutes of Metaphysics*, xii. 10.)

'If it could be admitted that matter and motion had an existence *in themselves*, or otherwise than as related to a consciousness, it would still not be by *such* matter and motion, but by the matter and motion which we know, that the functions of the soul, or anything else, can for us be explained. Nothing can be known by help of reference to the unknown. But matter and motion, just so far as known, consist in, or are determined by, relations between the objects of that connected consciousness which we call experience.... What then is the source of these relations ... the principle of union which renders them possible? Clearly it cannot itself be conditioned by any of the relations which result from its combining and unifying action. Being that which so organizes experience that the relations expressed by our definitions of matter and motion arise therein, it cannot itself be determined by those relations. It cannot be a matter or motion.' (T. H. Green, *Proleg. to Ethics*, c. i. § 9.)

NOTE 10. Page 52.

Personality a Mystery. Hartmann's *Philosophy of the Unconscious* contains much that is very suggestive on the 'unconscious' element in human personality, to which he considers that Leibniz was the first to call due attention.

'We attribute far too small dimensions to the rich empire of our Self, if we omit from it the unconscious region which resembles a great dark continent. The world which our memory peoples, only reveals in its revolution, a few luminous points at a time; while its immense and teeming mass remains in shade ... We daily see the conscious passing into unconsciousness; and take no notice of the bass accompaniment which our fingers continue to play, while our attention is directed to fresh musical effects.' (J. P. Richter, *Selina*, qu. by Hartmann, Introduction.)

Cf. also Schopenhauer's *World as Will and Idea*, though both these writers precisely invert the significance of the facts in question, by attributing them to Divine unconsciousness, instead of human limitation. Contrast the following passage from Lotze :—

'The finite being always works with powers with which it did not endow itself, and according to laws which it did not establish—that is, it works by means of a mental organization which is realized not only in it, but also in innumerable similar beings. Hence, in reflecting on self, it may easily seem to it as though there were in itself some obscure and unknown substance—something which is in the Ego though it is not the Ego itself, and to which, as to its subject, the whole personal development is attached. And hence there arise the questions—never to be quite silenced—What are we ourselves? What is our soul? What is our self—that obscure being, incomprehensible to ourselves, that stirs in our feelings and our passions, and never rises into complete self-consciousness? The fact that these questions can arise shows how far personality is from being developed in us to the extent which its notion admits and requires. It can be perfect only in the Infinite Being which, in surveying all its conditions or actions, never finds any content of that which it suffers or any law of its working, the meaning and origin of which are not transparently plain to it, and capable of being explained by reference to its own nature.' (Lotze, *Microcosmus*, ii. 9. 4.)

Cf. Newman's Sermon on 'The mysteriousness of our present being.' (*Par. Sermons*, vol. iv.)

LECTURE III

NOTE 11. Page 69.

Positive and Negative Theology. ''Ἐκ δύο γὰρ τούτων οἱονεὶ χαρακτήρ τις ἡμῖν ἐγγίνεται τοῦ Θεοῦ ἔκ τε τῆς τῶν ἀπεμφαινόντων ἀρνήσεως καὶ ἐκ τῆς τῶν ὑπαρχόντων ὁμολογίας.' (St. Basil, tom. i. *Adv. Eun.* I. 10.)

This distinction, which afterwards crystallized into positive and negative (καταφατική and ἀποφατική) theology, is constantly emphasized by the fathers and schoolmen; and in face of the crude objections which are often urged against dogma, it is important that its existence should be borne in mind. Patristic references to the subject will be found in Thomassin (*Theol. Dogm.* lib. iv.) who summarizes their teaching in the following passage:—

'Intexta implicataque sunt inter se haec omnia mysticae Patrum Theologiae capita; quod nil proprie de Deo intelligi aut dici possit, quod sciri possit quod sit, non quid sit; quod sciri possit quid non sit, non vero quid sit; quod affirmari de eo multa possint, imo omnia per modum causae, quod omnium causa sit; quod aequius sit eadem omnia de eo negare, quod causa sit longe praecellentissima, cujus vix tenuissimam umbram assequuntur omnes ab ea promanantes naturae; quod omnes negationes positionem aliquam implicent; non negantur enim de Deo quaelibet perfectiones, nisi ex sensu et conscientia perfectionis cujusdam longe eminentissimae, cujus hae sint extrema quaedam et fugientia vestigia; et vicissim positiones omnes de Deo ad negationes tandem resolvi debeant, propterea quod nil proprie sciri aut affirmari de divina essentia potest; quod denique natura divina majore intervallo superet naturas intellectuales, quam istae corporeas. Quocirca si corpora omnia corporeasque imagines amoliri necesse est, ut natura spiritalis mentium intelligatur; peraeque omnes mentium dotes removendae sunt, ut summa Dei natura intelligatur. (Thomassin, *Theol. Dogm.* lib. iv. 8. 1.)

See also, the 'Testimonies of Theologians' prefixed to the fifth edition of Mansel's *Bampton Lectures,* and id. lect. iv, notes 18 and 19.

For the ethical dangers to which an abstract use of the distinction may lead, cf. Dorner on Dionysius Areopagita. (*Person of Christ,* ii. 1. pp. 158 et seq., E. T.)

> 'Wer darf ihn nennen?
> Und wer bekennen:
> Ich glaub' ihn?
> Wer empfinden
> Und sich unterwinden,
> Zu sagen: ich glaub' ihn nicht?'
>
> (Goethe, *Faust.*)

NOTE 12. Page 74.

Personality legitimately predicable of God. The common objection—that since personality involves the contrast between an ego and a non-ego, a self and what is outside self, it cannot be predicated of God without implying that He is limited by something which is not Himself— is fully answered by Lotze, who maintains with undoubted truth, that we can clearly distinguish in thought between that immediate sense of self-existence which constitutes our Ego or self, and the various forms of the non-ego which are the conditions of its realization; and can conceive the latter, which do not constitute, but only call out the attributes of the Ego, to be necessary merely on account of our finite nature, and not inseparable from personality as such. He illustrates this by the analogy of the way in which a human person, as he gradually incorporates the results of external stimuli in his memory and character, becomes in a measure self-sufficing, and can produce much both of thought and action without recourse to the external world. Thus, what is 'only approximately possible for the finite mind, the conditioning of its life by itself, takes place without limit in God, and no contrast of an external world is necessary for Him.' The function of the non-ego, in short, on human personality, is not to define its circumference, but to stimulate its activity. And as any possible view of God involves His containing His own principle of activity; He can unquestionably be conceived as Personal without any reference beyond Himself. (See Lotze, *Microcosmus*, bk. ix. c. 4, and S. Harris, *Self-revelation of God*, pp. 174 et seq., 210 et seq.)

At the same time it is obvious that the Christian doctrine of the Trinity, with the possibilities of Divine self-determination which it involves, is a further assistance towards the conception of a Personality which is at once Infinite and yet definite. This thought is drawn out at great length by the obscure but suggestive writer Victorinus Afer (for whom see Thomassin, *Theol. Dogm. Tract.* ii. c. 32, and C. Gore, art. 'Victorinus' in Smith and Wace, *Dict. of Christian Biography*).

'Quod est esse, Pater est. Quod species Filius . . . Quom autem se videt, geminus existit et intelligitur;

videns, et quod videtur: ipse qui videt, ipsum quod videtur; quia se videt, hoc est igitur foras spectans, foris genitus vel existens, ut quid sit intelligat. Ergo si foris est, et sic genitus, Filius ... omnia ergo filius ut omnia pater.' (Vict. Afer, *Bibl. Patr.* iv. 1, pp. 188, 227, qu. by Thomassin.)

Cf. Irenaeus, 'Bene, qui dixit ipsum immensum Patrem in Filio mensuratum; mensura enim Patris Filius, quoniam et capit eum.' (*Haer.* iv. 2. 2.)

Also Origen: 'Πεπερασμένην γὰρ εἶναι καὶ τὴν δύναμιν τοῦ Θεοῦ λεκτέον, καὶ μὴ προφάσει εὐφημίας τὴν περιγραφὴν αὐτῆς περιαιρετέον· ἐὰν γὰρ ᾖ ἄπειρος ἡ θεία δύναμις, ἀνάγκη αὐτὴν μηδὲ ἑαυτὴν νοεῖν.' (*De Princip.* ii. 9.)

As we follow this train of thought, it becomes increasingly apparent that, as Lotze says, 'Perfect personality is in God alone.'

'It is not that human personality is a realized completeness to which we desire to make our conceptions of Divine Being correspond, but rather that human experience gives us indications of what Personality, in its fuller realization, would mean. Personality that lives only under material conditions in a world of dying, personality whose existence and origin are alike wholly independent of its own thought and will, and which only by degrees discovers a little as to the conditions of its own being—whatever rank it may hold in relation to other present phenomena—is plainly a most limited and imperfect form of personality. Only, then, the Supreme Being can attain the full idea of Personality. The ideals which hover behind and above human experience are suggestions, are approaches, more or less, towards that.' (R. C. Moberly, *Church Congress*, 1891.)

Cf. Augustine: 'Non audemus dicere unam essentiam,

tres substantias: sed unam essentiam vel substantiam, tres autem personas. Tamen cum quaeritur quid tres, magna prorsus inopia humanum laborat eloquium. Dictum est tamen tres personae, non ut illud diceretur, sed ne taceretur.' (*De Trin.* v. 9.)

Also St. Thomas Aquinas :—

'Persona significat id quod est perfectissimum in tota natura, sive subsistens in rationali natura. Unde, cum omne illud quod est perfectionis, Deo sit attribuendum, eo quod ejus essentia continet in se omnem perfectionem, conveniens est ut hoc nomen, persona, de Deo dicatur, non tamen eodem modo quo dicitur de creaturis; sed excellentiori modo: sicut et alia nomina quae creaturis a nobis imposita Deo attribuuntur.' (St. Thom. Aq. *Summa*, I. 29. 3.)

NOTE 13. Page 78.

Inadequate conceptions necessarily illusory, but not therefore delusive. 'What is the theological imagination of early times? It is essentially this—that man transports himself into nature—endues the great objects or powers of nature with human feeling, human will—and so prays and worships, and hopes to propitiate, and to obtain aid, compassion, deliverance. Well, this primitive imagination is *in the line of truth.* We begin with throwing a man's thought there into nature; we purify and exalt our imaginary being; we gradually release him from the grosser passions of mankind. We are, in fact, raising ourselves above the domination of those grosser passions; and as we grow wise and just, we make the good wise and just, beneficent and humane. Meanwhile science begins to show us this goodly whole as the creation of one Divine Artificer. And now we recognize, not without heart-beatings, that God is indeed not man, but that He has been educating man to comprehend Him in part, and to be in part like Him.

'Are not the Imagination and the Reason here strictly affiliated? We begin, as it has been boldly and truly said, by making God in our own image. What else could we do? Nature had not yet revealed herself to us in her great unity, as one whole, as the manifestation of one Power. We make God in our own image, but by-and-by, as our conceptions on every side enlarge, we find that it is God who is gradually elevating us by the expansion of our knowledge into some remote similitude with Himself. He is making us, in one sense, in His own image. This correspondence between the human and the Divine is the key-note of all religion; and Imagination, in her apparently wild and random way, had struck upon the note.

'God is making man in His own image, when He reveals to him the creation in its true nature, when He inspires him with a knowledge of the whole, and a love for the good of the whole. But the first step in this divine instruction was precisely the bold imagination by which man threw out into nature an image of himself. The form that imagination threw into the air was gradually modified and sublimed as man rose in virtue, and nature was better understood, till at length it harmonizes with, and merges into, a truth of the reason. Was man to wait for his God and his religion till his consciousness, in all other respects, was fully developed? Or was the revelation of the great truth to be sudden? Apparently not. Man *dreamt* a god first. But the dream was sent by the same Power, or came through the same law, that revealed the after-truth.' (W. Smith, *Thorndale*, v. ii. § 6.)

'The whole material world is a beneficent illusion to the intellect. . . . The very air that we breathe, and through the medium of which we see, cannot be trusted to present objects correctly to our sight. Even in the purest atmosphere the process of refraction must go on, and the sun must appear each day to rise before its time and with a slightly distorted orb. If, then, the different layers of our atmosphere, our medium of sight, have been so ordained by God that they shall always reveal to us the truth, yet leave part of the truth distorted or unrevealed, how is it unlikely that God may likewise have so constructed the several strata of the medium of His spiritual Revelation that the truth might be always more or less refracted and concealed, thus mercifully making us ever discontented with our modicum of knowledge, and, as we correct sight by the aid of Reason, so leading us to correct our interpretation of Revelation by the aid of Conscience.' (E. A. Abbot, *Through Nature to Christ*, v. 73.)

I venture to differ gravely from some of the conclusions which Dr. Abbot draws from this principle; chiefly in consequence of what I cannot but consider an unphilosophical view of the relation between what we call spirit, and matter; but his illustration of the principle itself and of its true bearing, is essentially important, in face of the popular tendency to treat the illusions of life as delusions, and base upon them pessimistic conclusions like those of Schopenhauer and Hartmann.

(Cf. also F. W. Robertson's Sermon on *The Illusiveness of Life*.)

LECTURE IV

NOTE 14. Page 81.

Theistic arguments. The patristic and scholastic arguments may be found in Petavius, Thomassin, or Suarez; and are examined in their modern reference by Kleutgen, *Philosophie der Vorzeit*; Gratry, *Connaissance de Dieu*.

Among more recent books may be mentioned, Flint's *Theism* (see also the references given in his note xxxvi. p. 423); Purinton's *Christian Theism*; Fisher's *Grounds of Theistic and Christian Belief* (chaps. i–iii); Ward's *Philosophy of Theism*; Martineau's *Study of Religion*; J. Caird's *Philosophy of Religion*; Ebrard's *Apologetics* (§§ 85–89, E. T.); Knight's *Aspects of Theism*; Bruce's *Apologetics*; Strong's *Manual of Theology*.

NOTE 15. Page 81.

The argument from the consensus gentium. In speaking of the common-sense philosophy, Hamilton remarks that 'the argument from common sense ... is not an appeal from philosophy to blind feeling. It is only an appeal from the heretical conclusions of particular philosophers, to the catholic principles of all philosophy.' (Reid's *Works*, note A. § 3.) And the same may be said of the Theistic argument from universal consent, which is in fact a special application, or departmental section of the same great principle.

The fact discovered by induction that man (with insignificant exceptions) is everywhere and always religious, may be legitimately translated into the inference that man is instinctively, i.e. naturally or constitutionally, religious; in the sense in which St. Thomas says, 'Dei cognitio nobis innata dicitur esse, in quantum per principia nobis innata de facili percipere possumus Deum esse' (Opusc. 70 super Boeth. *de Trin.*), and accordingly we find the argument stated in both these forms. It would appear to have had influence even with Epicurus. 'Solus enim (Epicurus) vidit, primum esse deos quod in omnium animis eorum notionem impressisset ipsa natura. Quae est enim gens aut quod genus hominum quod non habeat sine doctrina anticipationem quandam deorum.' (Cic. N. D. qu. by Zeller, *Stoics and Epicureans*, c. xviii. note.) And its frequent use by the earlier fathers is, as Kleutgen points out, of especial significance, from their wide acquaintance with the pagan life and literature of their time. Cf. passages quoted in Kleutgen (*Philos. der Vorzeit*), and Hagenbach (*History of Christian Doctrine*, § 35, E. T.) e.g.

'Τὸ Θεὸς ... πράγματος δυσεξηγήτου ἔμφυτος τῇ φύσει τῶν ἀνθρώπων δόξα.' (Justin, *Apol.* ii. 6.)

'Πᾶσιν γὰρ ἁπαξαπλῶς ἀνθρώποις ... ἐνέστακταί τις ἀπόρροια θεϊκή.' (Clem. Alex. *Coh.* vi. 59.) Other of his phrases are 'ἔμφασις φυσικὴ—ἐμφύτως καὶ ἀδιδάκτως.'

'Πᾶσι γὰρ ἡ γνῶσις τοῦ εἶναι θεὸν ὑπ' αὐτοῦ φυσικῶς ἐγκατέσπαρται.' (John Damasc. *De Fid. Or.* i. 1.)

'Quod colimus deus unus est ... vultis ex animae ipsius testimonio comprobemus? quae licet carcere corporis pressa ... quum tamen resipiscit ... et sanitatem suam patitur, deum nominat, hoc solo, quia proprie verus hic unus. ... O testimonium animae naturaliter Christianae.' (Tert. *Apol.* c. 17; cf. *De Test. An.* c. 1.)

Modern investigation, as stated in the text, has immensely strengthened the inductive basis of this argument. See the works there quoted; also Flint's *Theism*, note 8, and the references there given.

NOTE 16. Page 84.

The cosmological argument. The kernel of this argument in all its forms, is that we have a positive notion of unconditioned or independent being. Such being is a presupposition of all our consciousness; something which on reflection we find to lie at the root of our perceptions as well as our conceptions, and which thus guarantees its own reality. We discover—we do not infer—that it exists, and exists as positive and concrete. This is well stated in the following passages.

'The conception of unconditioned being is given us, whether delusively or not, by the senses themselves; every stable object stands out at first complete in itself, and every agent acts apparently with a power of its own; we learn from observation and experiment that it is otherwise. The conceptions of unconditioned being and power are driven out of the material world to find their place in theology. Take, for illustration, the idea of Absolute Rest.... It was a favourite expression of some of the ancient philosophers, that God "was the cause of all motion, but partook of none." Modern philosophers do not use this expression, but no one can object to it on the ground that we have not the idea of absolute rest, or that, because it is nowhere in the world, it may not be exemplified in God. Such ideas as those of eternal permanence, unconditioned being, self-originating act or power, are found to be misplaced when applied to anything in the arena of ever-moving, changeful and conditioned existence; but show us that there is a legitimate arena for these ideas (as is done by demonstrating the necessary pre-existence of the idea of the whole), and we forthwith transfer them to that arena.' (William Smith, *Thorndale*, p. 440.)

'Everything of which his senses cannot perceive a limit, is to a primitive savage, or to any man in an early stage of intellectual activity, unlimited or infinite. Man sees, he sees to a certain point; and there his eyesight breaks down. But exactly where his eyesight breaks down, there presses upon him, whether he likes it or not, the perception of the unlimited or the infinite. It may be said that this is not perception, in the ordinary sense of the word. No more it is, but still less is it mere reasoning. In perceiving the infinite, we neither count, nor measure, nor compare, nor name. We know not what it is, but we know that it is, and we know it, because we actually feel it and are brought in contact with it. If it seems too bold to say that man actually sees the invisible, let us say that he suffers from the invisible, and this invisible is only a special name for the infinite. . . . The infinite, therefore, instead of being merely a late abstraction, is really implied in the earliest manifestations of our sensuous knowledge.' (Max Müller, *Hibbert Lectures*, i. 37.)

'The true idea of the infinite is not a negation nor a modification of any other idea. The finite, on the contrary, is in reality the limitation or modification of the infinite, nor is it possible, if we reason in good earnest, to conceive of the finite in any other sense than as a shadow of the infinite.' (Id. *Lect. on Lang.* ii. p. 596. Cf. *Natural Religion*, p. 125; *Anthropological*

Religion, p. 106.)   Cf. also McCosh, *Intuitions of Mind*, pp. 214–30.

Historically the argument dates from Plato and Aristotle. It is used by Diodorus of Tarsus (qu. by Hagenbach, *H. of D.* § 123), by Boëthius, and continually by the schoolmen, e. g.

'Omne.., quod imperfectum esse dicitur, id diminutione perfecti imperfectum esse perhibetur. Quo fit, ut si in quolibet genere imperfectum quid esse videatur, in eo perfectum quoque aliquid esse necesse sit. Etenim perfectione sublata, unde illud quod imperfectum perhibetur extiterit, ne fingi quidem potest. Neque enim a diminutis inconsummatisque natura rerum cepit exordium, sed ab integris absolutisque procedens, in haec extrema atque effoeta dilabitur.' (Boëthius, *De Consol. Phil.* iii. 10.)

'Quicquid est per aliud, minus est quam illud, per quod cuncta sunt alia et quod solum est per se: quare illud, quod est per se, maxime omnium est. Est igitur unum aliquid, quod solum maxime et summe omnium est.' (Anselm, *Monol.* iii.)

'Ex illo esse quod non est ab aeterno nec a semet ipso ratiocinando colligitur et illud esse quod est a semet ipso et eo quidem etiam ab aeterno. Nam si nihil a semet ipso fuisset non esset omnino unde ea existere potuissent, quae suum esse a semet ipsis non habent nec habere valent.' (R. de St. Victor, *De Trin.* 18.)

It is given in three aspects by St. Thom. Aq.: 'Probatur per motum dari primum movens, secundo primum efficiens, tertio semper aliquid fuit quod est necessarium et non possibile' (*Summ.* 1, 2, 3); and lies at the root of all the philosophy of the seventeenth century, e. g.

'Dum in me ipsum mentis aciem converto, non modo

intelligo me esse rem incompletam et ab alio dependentem remque ad majora et majora sive meliora indefinite aspirantem, sed *simul etiam* intelligo illum a quo pendeo majora ista omnia non indefinite et potentia tantum, sed reipsa infinite in se habere atque ita Deum esse, totaque vis argumenti in eo est quod agnoscam fieri non posse ut existam talis naturae, qualis sum, nempe ideam Dei in me habens, nisi re vera Deus etiam existeret.' (Descartes, *Medit.* 3.)

'Quas absolute format infinitatem exprimunt. . . . Ideas positivas prius format quam negativas.' (Spinoza, *De Intel. Emend.* xv. 108.)

'Tout ce que l'esprit aperçoit immédiatement et directement est ou existe . . . j'aperçois immédiatement et directement l'infini. Donc il est.' (Malebranche, *Entret. d'un phil. chrét.* p. 365.)

'Qu'est-ce qui a mis l'idée de l'infini dans un sujet si borné? . . . Supposons que l'esprit de l'homme est comme un miroir . . . Quel être a pu mettre en nous *l'image* de l'infini, si l'infini ne fut jamais? . . . Cette image de l'infini, c'est le vrai infini dont nous avons la pensée. . . . S'il n'était pas, pourrait-il se graver au fond de notre esprit? . . . Dieu, est véritablement en lui-même tout ce qu'il y a de réel et de positif dans les esprits, tout ce qu'il y a de réel et de positif dans les corps, tout ce qu'il y a de réel et de positif dans les essences de toutes les créatures possibles, dont je n'ai point d'idée distincte. Il a tout l'être du corps, sans être borné au corps; tout l'être de l'esprit, sans être borné à l'esprit; et de même des autres essences possibles. Il est tellement tout être, qu'il a tout l'être de chacune de ces créatures, mais en retranchant la borne qui la restreint. Otez toute borne; ôtez toute différence qui resserre l'être dans les espèces;

vous demeurez dans l'universalité de l'être, et, par conséquent, dans la perfection infinie de l'Être par lui-même.' (Fénelon, *Traité de l'Exist de Dieu*, i. ii. 53 ; ii. v. 66.) For the fuller treatment of it, see Gratry, *Connaissance de Dieu*, passim. And for its criticism, E. Caird, *Philosophy of Kant*.

NOTE 17. Page 93.

The Teleological argument. This argument falls naturally into two divisions: use and beauty; of which latter Mozley says (*Sermon on Nature*): 'When the materialist has exhausted himself in efforts to explain utility in nature, it would appear to be the peculiar office of beauty to rise up suddenly as a confounding and baffling *extra*, which was not even formally provided for in his scheme. . . . Physical science goes back and back into nature, but it is the aspect and front of nature which gives the challenge; and it is a challenge which no backward train of physical causes can meet.'

It should be noticed that this aesthetic aspect of the argument from design is that to which the Fathers, with their evidently intense appreciation of nature, chiefly appeal, e. g.

'Οὐδὲ χρὴ τὰ τοιαῦτα πειρᾶσθαι ἀποδεικνύναι, φανερᾶς οὔσης τῆς θείας προνοίας ἔκ τε τῆς ὄψεως τῶν ὁρωμένων πάντων τεχνικῶν καὶ σοφῶν ποιημάτων, καὶ τῶν μὲν τάξει γινομένων τῶν δὲ τάξει φανερουμένων.' (S. Clem. Alex. *Strom.* v.)

'Τοῦ μὲν γὰρ εἶναι Θεὸν καὶ τὴν πάντων ποιητικήν τε καὶ συνεκτικὴν αἰτίαν καὶ ὄψις διδάσκαλος καὶ ὁ φυσικὸς νόμος· ἡ μὲν τοῖς ὁρωμένοις προσβάλλουσα καὶ πεπηγόσι καλῶς καὶ ὁδεύουσι καὶ ἀκινήτως, ἵνα οὕτως εἴπω, κινουμένοις καὶ φερομένοις· ὁ δὲ διὰ τῶν ὁρωμένων καὶ τεταγμένων τὸν ἀρχηγὸν τούτων συλλογιζόμενος.' (St. Greg. Naz. *Orat.* 28. n. 6.)

'... ἔστι πάλιν καὶ ἀπὸ τῶν φαινομένων τὴν περὶ τοῦ Θεοῦ γνῶσιν καταλαβεῖν, τῆς κτίσεως ὥσπερ γράμμασι διὰ τῆς τάξεως καὶ ἁρμονίας τὸν ἑαυτῆς δεσπότην καὶ ποιητὴν σημαινούσης καὶ βοώσης.' (St. Athan. *Ad Gen.* 34.)

'Ἐκ μεγέθους καὶ καλλονῆς κτισμάτων ἀναλόγως ὁ γενεσιουργὸς θεωρεῖται.' (Id. *Ib.* 44.)

'Deum quippe Patrem ex magnitudine et pulchritudine creaturarum potest quis intelligere, et a conditionibus conditor consequenter agnoscitur.' (St. Jerom. *In Gal.* 3, 2.)

'Quis mundum intuens Deum esse non sentiat?' (St. Hilar. *In Psalm.* 52.)

For further quotations, which might be multiplied indefinitely, see Landriot, *Le Christ de la Tradition*, and Hagenbach, *H. of Doctrine*.

The later schoolmen would seem to have thought more of the utilitarian aspect of design, and hence laid themselves open to the attacks of Bacon and Spinoza. Cf.

'Necessitas naturalis inhaerens rebus, qua determinantur ad unum est impressio quaedam Dei dirigentis ad finem.., necessitas naturalis creaturarum demonstrat divinae providentiae gubernationem.' (St. Thom. *Summ.* i. 103, a. 1.)

'Naturalia tendunt in fines determinatos.... Quum ergo ipsa non praestituant sibi finem, quia rationem finis non cognoscunt, oportet quod eis praestituatur finis ab alio, qui sit naturae institutor. Hic autem est, qui praebet omnibus esse et est per se necesse esse, quem Deum dicimus. Non autem posset naturae finem praestituere nisi intelligeret. Deus igitur est intelligens.' (Id. *Contr. Gent.* i. 43. 6.)

The real strength of the argument consists in the way in which, as pointed out by Mozley, these two absolutely independent things are inextricably interwoven. 'Nature, while she labours at her work, sleeps like a picture;' a fact which is fatal to dysteleology. For modern treatments of the question, see Janet, *Final Causes;* (E. T.) Hartmann's *Philosophy of the Unconscious* (whose array of facts may be safely trusted to refute his inferences); Le Conte, *Evolution;* Mozley, *Essay on Design* and *Sermon on Nature;* Ebrard's *Apologetics*, §§ 144-155; Flint (esp. Notes 13-21); J. Croll, *The Philosophical Basis of Evolution* (esp. c. 19); *Riddles of the Sphinx* (c. 7, §§ 17-22).

NOTE 18. Page 102.

The Ontological Argument. This argument, which might perhaps best be described as the argument from the reality of thought, must be distinguished from the cosmological argument which in fact it underlies, but with which it has often been confused in statement. Anselm, for instance, runs the two into each other, and is neither the first nor the best exponent of the Ontological argument, with which he is sometimes exclusively credited. St. Augustine is its best early exponent in his treatise, *De libro arbitrio.* The following quotation will illustrate his reasoning, though it is somewhat diffuse and difficult to condense.

'Si quid melius quam id quod in mea natura optimum est (sc. ratio) invenire potuero Deum esse dixerim. . . . Nullo modo negaveris esse incommutabilem veritatem haec omnia quae incommutabiliter vera sunt continentem, quam non possis dicere tuam vel meam, vel cuiusquam hominis, sed omnibus incommutabilia vera cernentibus, tanquam miris modis secretum et publicum lumen, praesto esse ac se praebere communiter: omne autem quod communiter omnibus ratiocinantibus atque intelligentibus praesto est, ad ullius eorum proprie naturam pertinere quis dixerit?... Promiseram autem, si meministi, me tibi demonstraturum esse aliquid, quod sit mente nostra atque ratione sublimius. Ecce tibi est ipsa veritas.... Tu autem concesseras, si quid supra mentes nostras esse monstrarem, Deum te esse confessurum, si adhuc nihil esset superius.... Si... aliquid est excellentius, ille potius Deus est: si autem non est, iam ipsa veritas Deus est.' (Aug. *De lib. arb.* ii. 14–39.)

Cf. Anselm, 'Cum veritas quae est in rerum existentia sit effectus summae veritatis, ipsa quoque causa est veritatis quae cognitionis est, et eius quae est in propositione.' (*De Ver.* ix.)

'Ex superioribus habemus quod ipsa sapientia idem sit quod divina substantia.' (R. de St. Victor, *De Trin.* i. 22.)

Cf. the following modern statements:

'The ontological argument — the argument from thought to being—when relieved of its imperfect syllogistic... form, is simply the expression of that highest unity of thought and being, which all knowledge presupposes as its beginning and seeks as its end. Idealism, in the sense that all things and beings constitute a system of relations which finds its unity in mind, that every intelligence contains in it the form of the universe, and that, therefore, all knowledge is but the discovery of that which is already our own—the awaking of a self-consciousness, which involves at the same time a consciousness of God—*this* idealism is the real meaning of the ontological argument, and the only meaning in which it is defensible.' (E. Caird, *Crit. Phil. of Kant*, ii. 13.)

'The real pre-supposition of all knowledge, or the thought which is the *prius* of all things, is not the individual's consciousness of himself as individual, but a thought or self-consciousness which is beyond all individual selves, which is the unity of all individual selves and their objects, of all thinkers and all objects of thought. Or, to put it differently, when we are compelled to think of all existences as relative to thought, and of thought as prior to all, amongst the existences to which it is prior is our own individual self. We can make our individual self, just as much as other things, the object of thought. We can not only think, but we can think the individual thinker. We might even say that, strictly speaking, it is not we that think, but the universal reason that thinks in us. In other words, in thinking, we rise to a universal point of view, from which our individuality is of no more account than the individuality of any other object. Hence, as thinking beings, we dwell already in a region in which our individual feelings and opinions, as such, have no absolute worth, but that which alone has absolute worth is a thought which does not pertain to us individually, but is the universal life of all intelligences, or the life of universal, absolute intelligence.

'What, then, we have thus reached as the true meaning of the ontological proof is this: that, as spiritual beings, our whole conscious life is based on a universal self-consciousness, an absolute spiritual life, which is not a mere subjective notion or conception, but which carries with it the proof of its necessary existence or reality.' (J. Caird, *Introd. to Phil. of Rel.* v. § 3.)

Cf. E. Caird, *Kant,* chap. xiii. and Green's *Prolegomena to Ethics,* §§ 26 et seq.; W. T. Harris, *Hegel's Logic,* chap. xxxi.

NOTE 19. Page 103.

The Moral Argument. 'It is the circumstance that man is possessed of a distinct will which suggests the idea that God is not a mere law or principle, but a person with a power of voluntary determination. It is in consequence of his possessing an inherent and positive freedom that man is led to look upon God as also free, and this in a higher and more absolute sense, inasmuch as there can be nothing to lay restraint upon his liberty. May we not go a step further, and maintain that the possession of voluntary power and freedom on the part of man, is not only fitted to suggest, but is a proof, that the God from whom they proceeded has a will, and that this will is free.' (McCosh, *Intuitions of the Mind,* p. 453.)

This argument is powerfully stated by Cardinal Newman.

'It is obvious that Conscience is the essential principle and sanction of religion in the mind. Conscience implies a relation between the soul and a something exterior, and that, moreover, superior to itself; a relation to an excellence which it does not possess, and to a tribunal over which it has no power. And since the more closely this inward monitor is respected and followed, the clearer, the more exalted, and the more varied its dictates become, and the standard of excellence is ever outstripping, while it guides our obedience, a moral conviction is thus at length obtained of the unapproachable nature, as well as the supreme authority of That, whatever it is, which is the object of the mind's contemplation. Here, then, at once, we have the elements of a religious system; for what is religion but the system of relations existing between us and a Supreme Power, claiming our habitual obedience.' (Newman's *University Sermons*, ii.)

'Conscience . . . is something more than a moral sense . . . it always implies what that sense only sometimes implies . . . the recognition of a living object, towards which it is directed. Inanimate things cannot stir our affections; these are correlative with persons. If, as is the case, we feel responsibility, are ashamed, are frightened, at transgressing the voice of conscience, this implies that there is One to whom we are responsible, before whom we are ashamed, whose claims upon us we fear. If, on doing wrong, we feel the same tearful, broken-hearted sorrow which overwhelms us on hurting a mother; if, on doing right, we enjoy the same sunny serenity of mind, the same soothing, satisfactory delight which follows on our receiving praise from a father, we certainly have within us the image of some person, to whom our love and veneration look, in whose smile we find our happiness, for whom we yearn, towards whom we direct our pleadings, in whose anger we are troubled and waste away. These feelings in us are such as require for their exciting cause an intelligent being: we are not affectionate towards a stone, nor do we feel shame before a horse or a dog; we have no remorse or compunction on breaking mere human law: yet, so it is, conscience excites all these painful emotions, confusion, foreboding, self-condemnation; and, on the other hand, it sheds upon us a deep peace, a sense of security, a resignation, and a hope, which there is no sensible, no earthly object to elicit. "The wicked flees, when no one pursueth": then why does he flee? whence his terror? Who is it that he sees in solitude, in darkness, in the hidden chambers of his heart? If the cause of these emotions does not belong to this visible world, the object to which his perception is directed must be Supernatural and Divine.' (*Grammar of Assent*, p. 107.)

It may be interesting to notice that the relation between this and the Teleological argument, of which so much has been made since Kant, is forcibly expressed by Raymond of Sabunde, e.g.

'Quoniam homo, in quantum homo, est talis naturae, quod facit opera sua talia ad quae de natura sua sequitur meritum vel demeritum, et per consequens debetur eis praemium vel poena . . . necesse est quod sit aliquis supra hominem maior, qui possit hoc remunerare vel punire, et correspondere sibi secundum opera sua. Si enim non esset aliquis, qui posset hoc facere, sequeretur quod homo esset frustra et in vanum, quia opera eius essent frustra, quia ultra alia opera aliarum rerum sunt praemialia et punibilia, et si nullus sit qui correspondeat operibus suis praemiando, sequitur, quod totum universum est frustra et inordinatum, quia omnia inferiora serviunt homini, et sunt propter hominem, et homo est pars principalis universi. Et si homo est frustra, sequitur, quod totum residuum est frustra. Et tamen videmus ad sensum, quod omnia inferiora usque ad hominem sunt ordinata, et tamen homo non ordinavit illa. Sequitur ergo, quod etiam homo erit ordinatus. Et etiam sequitur quod aliquis respondebit homini secundum eius naturam.' (Raymond de Sabunde, *T. Nat.* Tit. 83.)

'Homo in quantum homo habet liberum arbitrium, per quod facit opera meritoria seu demeritoria. Et ideo necesse est, quod in natura sit aliquis praemiator vel punitor: ... hoc autem clamat totum universum, cuius homo principalior pars existit: et etiam opera hominum hoc requirunt, qui volunt habere debitum, scil. poenum vel praemium.' (Id., Tit. 86.)

In this connexion it is important to recognize the unquestionable primacy assigned by Kant to the practical reason, as he is sometimes misrepresented on the point.

'The doctrine of freedom, and the absolute supremacy of the moral order of the world, or the doctrine of the primacy of practical reason, rests with Kant upon firm ground. The moral proof for the existence of God stands or falls with this doctrine. Regarding the *theoretical* demonstrability of God's existence, Kant held different views at different stages of his philosophical inquiry. . . . But, however differently he may have thought on this point—namely, the *knowableness* of God—there was not a moment in the course of the development of his philosophical convictions when he denied, or even only doubted, the *reality* of God.' (Kuno Fischer's *Critique of Kant*, c. ii. § 3, E. T.)

'We have to remember that the *Critique of Pure Reason*, after all, is only the first stage in the process of Kant's thought, and that its main value is to prepare the way for the second stage, which is contained in the *Critique of Practical Reason*. If knowledge of the objects of the Ideas of reason is denied by Kant to be possible, it is only to make room for faith. We can *think* the noumenal, and we can *believe* in it, though we *know* only the phenomenal. And this exclusion of knowledge, if, in one aspect of it, it means the limitation of our intelligence, as capable only of understanding that which is given to it through sense, in another aspect of it, points to the infinity of our nature, as subjects who are conscious of themselves, and who, as so conscious, are not subjected to the limitations which they impose on all the objects they know. The limitation of knowledge to phenomena is thus the liberation of the noumena, and especially of the noumenal subject, from the conditions to which all phenomenal objects are subjected. Experience is not a closed circle; for the very principles on which it rests point to something that is not included within it; and alongside of the realm of nature and necessity, or rather as an opposite counterpart to it, Kant forthwith proceeds to set up the realm of morality and freedom.' (E. Caird, *Philosophy of Kant*, ii. p. 141. Cf. also i. pp. 228 et seq.)

LECTURE V.

NOTE 20. Page 129.

Morality the condition of spiritual insight. 'Γενέσθω δὴ πρῶτον θεοειδὴς πᾶς εἰ μέλλει θεάσασθαι θεόν τε καὶ καλόν.' (Plotinus, *Enn.* i. 6. 9.)

'Fideli menti multae undique rationes occurrunt, multa denique argumenta emergunt.' (R. de St. Victor, *De Cont.* 3.)

'Vera fides liberat et magnificat ipsum intellectum,

quia non constringit eum intra terminos, intra quos ratio habet eum terminatum.' (R. Lulli, *De Con. Dei*, x. 36.)

Cf. passages qu. by Hagenbach (*H. of Doct.* § 35. 7.)

This principle should be too axiomatic to need statement, but is in fact continually ignored in popular controversy. The following statements from grave reasoners may, therefore, be worth quoting.

''Tis not, therefore, for want of sufficient evidence that men disbelieve the great truths of religion; but plainly for want of integrity, and of dealing ingenuously and impartially with themselves.' (Clarke, *Evidences*, p. xv. Cf. *Being and Attributes*, ad init.)

'Inattention, among us, to revealed religion, will be found to imply the same dissolute immoral temper of mind, as inattention to natural religion.' (Butler, *Analogy*, Conclusion.)

LECTURE VI

NOTE 21. Page 155.

Primitive man. The theory of evolution has raised questions respecting the primitive condition of man, which had never occurred to earlier thinkers. For passages bearing on the theological treatment of the subject, cf. Hagenbach (*Hist. of Christian Doct.* §§ 61, 175, 245). It will be noticed that some of the earlier writers are much freer and more philosophical on the point than the later; e. g. Origen, ''Εν τοῖς δοκοῦσι περὶ τοῦ 'Αδὰμ εἶναι φυσιολογεῖ Μωϋσῆς τὰ περὶ τῆς τοῦ ἀνθρώπου φύσεως.' (*Cont. Cels.* iv. 40.) While, among the later, the unwarranted position referred to in the text is more common among the Protestant writers, whose tendency to exaggerate the effects of the fall, led them also to exaggerate the elevation of the unfallen state. With these contrast the language of Bellarmine: 'Non magis differt status hominis post lapsum Adae a statu eiusdem in puris naturalibus, quam differt spoliatus a nudo, neque deterior est humana natura, si culpam originalem detrahas, neque magis ignorantia et infirmitate laborat, quam esset et laboraret in puris naturalibus condita.' (*De Gratia*, tom. iv. c. 2, Pr. 4.)

NOTE 22. Page 162.

Natural Religion. (Christianity) 'is a religion in addition to the religion of nature; it does not supersede or contradict it; it recognizes and depends on it, and that of necessity: for how possibly can it prove its claims except by an appeal to what men have already? be it ever so miraculous, it cannot dispense with nature; this would be to cut the ground from under it; for what would be the worth of evidence in favour of a revelation which denied the authority of that system of thought, and those methods of reasoning, out of which those evidences necessarily grew?' (Newman's *Grammar of Assent*, p. 383.)

Cf. Augustine. 'Res ipsa quae nunc Christiana religio nuncupatur, erat apud antiquos, nec defuit ab initio generis humani, quousque ipse Christus veniret in carnem, unde vera religio quae iam erat coepit appellari Christiana.' (*Retract.* i. 12. 3.)

The translation of the *Sacred Books of the East* (ed. M. Müller) will enable the ordinary reader to form a fairer estimate of the oriental religions—their weakness, and their strength—than can possibly be gathered from any manual or summary, or collection of elegant extracts.

Cf. also the various *Hibbert* and *Gifford Lectures*, Robertson Smith's *Religion of the Semites* (and, in connexion with the latter, Fraser's *Golden Bough*). For a Bibliography, see Tiele's *Outlines*, and Schrader's *Manual*.

For a comparison between Christianity and other religions, see Hardwick, *Christ and other Masters* (which would require modifications in the present day); Wordsworth, *Bampton Lectures, The One Religion*; Copleston, *Buddhism in Ceylon*.

LECTURE VII

NOTE 23. Page 172.

Ethnic Inspiration. For numerous passages illustrating the Indian and Greek views of Inspiration, see Muir, *Sanskrit Texts*, vol. iii. c. 2. The principle upon which the recognition of such inspiration rests, is stated by Cardinal Newman in the following passage:

'When religion of some sort is said to be *natural*, it is not meant that any religious system has been actually traced out by unaided Reason. We know of no such system, because we know of no time or country in which human Reason *was* unaided. Scripture informs us that revelations were granted to the first fathers of our race, concerning the nature of God and man's duty to Him;

and scarcely a people can be named, among whom there are not traditions, not only of the existence of powers exterior to this visible world, but also of their actual interference with the course of nature, followed up by religious communications to mankind from them. The Creator has never left Himself without such witness as might anticipate the conclusions of Reason, and support a wavering conscience and perplexed faith. No people (to speak in general terms) has been denied a revelation from God, though but a portion of the world has enjoyed an authenticated revelation.' (Newman's *University Sermons*, ii.)

Cf. Bede: 'In quantum vero vel gustum aliquem sapientiae cuiuslibet vel virtutis imaginem habebant totum hoc desuper acceperunt; non solum munere primae conditionis, verum etiam quotidiana eius gratia, qui creaturam suam nec se deserentem deserens, dona sua, prout ipse iudicaverit hominibus et magna magnis et parva largitur parvis.' (*Exp. in Cant. Cant.*, Opp. ix. 197.)

LECTURE VIII

NOTE 24. Page 192.

The Incarnation. It has been impossible, within the compass of the present lectures, to do more than indicate in outline the relation of the Incarnation to their general argument. But this deficiency may be more than supplemented by reference to the treatment of the subject in the *Bampton Lectures* for 1891. (C. Gore, *The Incarnation*.)

The following passage contains a concise summary of the argumentative position:

'The evidence for the authority of Jesus Christ is essentially of a cumulative character; ... we decline to consider any portion of it in entire isolation from the rest. It is true that when He entered on His work, and made His first appeal to one nation, He based that appeal very largely on the Scriptures of the earlier Dispensation. But even then His fulfilling of the Scriptures, His concentration in His Person, and His teaching of every ray which had enlightened His Jewish ancestors, did not constitute more than a small portion of the evidence which convinced His first followers; the appeal of those first followers to the Gentile world of their day travelled far beyond the narrower region of His fulfilment of the earlier Dispensation; the Roman world submitted itself to Him on the ground of the correspondence of His work, of the appeal of His Death and Resurrection, of the exact adaptation of His teaching to primary needs of human nature, independent altogether of the Jewish Scriptures; and our own belief in Him and His Religion appeals, again, to what I would call with all reverence, His actual, historical contribution to the advance of human progress, to the permanence of all that He has done for human life under aspects the most varied, individual, national, world-wide; to His ability tested through the centuries, to supply every need of humanity—whether those of individual souls in the spiritual wants of their inmost being, or those of society at large, on the highest scale of its organization. It is by taking all these things into account that we arrive at our belief in His Person.' (*Churchmen and the Higher Criticism*: a Charge, by L. G. Mylne, Bishop of Bombay: Bombay, 1893.)

NOTE 25. Page 193.

The supernatural dignity of man. 'The earth is a point not only in respect of the heavens above us, but of that heavenly and celestial part within us. That mass of flesh that circumscribes me limits not my mind. That surface that tells the heavens it hath an end cannot persuade me that I have any.... Whilst I study to find how I am a microcosm or little body, I find myself something more than the great. There is surely a piece of divinity in us; something that was before the elements, and pays no homage to the sun. Nature tells me I am the image of God, as well as scripture.' (Sir Thomas Browne, *Rel. Med.*)

Cf. Pascal. 'Tous les corps, le firmament, les étoiles, la terre et les royaumes, ne valent pas le moindre des esprits, car il connoît tout cela, et soi-même; et le corps, rien. Et tous les corps, et tous les esprits ensemble, et toutes leurs productions, ne valent pas le moindre mouvement de charité, car elle est d'un ordre infiniment plus élevé. De tous les corps ensemble on ne sauroit tirer la moindre pensée : cela est impossible, et d'un autre ordre. Tous les corps et les esprits ensemble ne sauroient produire un mouvement de vraie charité : cela est impossible, et d'un autre ordre tout surnaturel.' (*Pensées*, ii. 10. 1.) Cf. Browning (*Paracelsus*, pp. 185–192.)

'All tended to mankind,
And, man produced, all has its end thus far:
But in completed man begins anew
A tendency to God. Pronostics told
Man's near approach; so in man's self arise

August anticipations, symbols, types
Of a dim splendour ever on before
In that eternal circle life pursues.'

Such statements may be called rhetorical, but rhetoric in this case merely means the emotional statement of a rational conviction. This conviction, as argued in the text, is the necessary presupposition of the Incarnation. 'He is worthy that Thou shouldest do this for him'; and was so regarded by the Fathers, who continually emphasize the thought of man being created in the image and likeness of God. Cf. passages in Hagenbach (*H. of D.* § 56).

NOTE 26. Page 211.

The conceptions of Divine and human personality vary together. 'Belief in the personality of man and belief in the personality of God stand or fall together. A glance at the history of religion would suggest that these two beliefs are for some reason inseparable. Where faith in the personality of God is weak, or is altogether wanting, as in the case of the pantheistic religions of the East, the perception which men have of their own personality is found to be, in an equal degree, indistinct. The feeling of individuality is dormant. The soul indolently ascribes to itself a merely phenomenal being. It conceives of itself as appearing for a moment, like a wavelet on the ocean, to vanish again in the all-ingulfing essence whence it emerged. Recent philosophical theories which substitute matter, or an "Unknowable," for the self-conscious Deity, likewise dissipate the personality of man as ordinarily conceived. If they deny that God is a Spirit, they deny with equal emphasis that man is a spirit. The pantheistic and atheistic schemes are in this respect consistent in their logic; but of man's perception of his own personal attributes, arises the belief in a personal God. On this fact of our own personality the validity of the arguments for theism depends.' (G. P. Fisher, *The Grounds of Theistic and Christian Belief*, p. 1.)

NOTE 27. Page 214.

Psychological illustrations of the doctrine of the Trinity. Numerous physical illustrations of the Trinity are employed by the Fathers (for which see Thomassin, *Theol. Dogm.*, Tract ii. c. 26), but they can never be pressed, without risk of passing into Sabellianism; whereas the psychological illustrations, which are obviously the more fundamental, have no such attendant danger. Cf. passages quoted in Hagenbach (*H. of C. D.*, §§ 42, 43), to which the following may be added.

'"Ωσπερ δὲ τὸν Λόγον ἐκ τῶν καθ' ἡμᾶς ἀναλογικῶς ἐπὶ τῆς ὑπερκειμένης ἔγνωμεν φύσεως, κατὰ τὸν αὐτὸν τρόπον καὶ τῇ περὶ τοῦ Πνεύματος ἐννοίᾳ προσαχθησόμεθα σκιάς τινας καὶ μιμήματα τῆς ἀφράστου δυνάμεως ἐν τῇ καθ' ἡμᾶς θεωροῦντες φύσει.' (Greg. Nys. *Orat. Cat.* 2.)

'Ante omnia Deus erat solus... quia nihil aliud extrinsecus praeter illum. Ceterum ne tunc quidem solus; habebat enim secum quam habebat in semetipso rationem, suam scilicet.... Quae ratio sensus ipsius est. Hanc Graeci λόγον dicunt, quo vocabulo etiam sermonem appellamus.... Idque quo facilius intellegas ex teipso ante recognosce.... Vide cum tacitus tecum ipse congrederis ratione, hoc ipsum agi intra te, occurrente ea tibi cum sermone ad omnem cogitatus tui motum, ad omnem sensus tui pulsum. . . . Ita secundus quodammodo in te est sermo, per quem loqueris cogitando, et per quem cogitas loquendo; ipse sermo alius est. Quanto ergo plenius hoc agitur in Deo . . . quod habeat in se etiam tacendo rationem, et in ratione sermonem? . . . quem secundum a se faceret agitando intra se.' (Tert. *Adv. Prax.* c. v.)

'Nos quidem in nobis, tametsi non aequalem, imo valde longeque distantem, neque coaeternum, et quo brevius totum dicitur, non eiusdem substantiae, cuius est Deus, tamen qua Deo nihil sit in rebus ab eo factis natura propinquius, imaginem Dei, hoc est summae illius Trinitatis, agnoscimus, adhuc reformatione perficiendum, ut sit etiam similitudine proxima. Nam et sumus, et nos esse novimus, et id (nostrum) esse ac nosse diligimus. In his autem tribus quae dixi, nulla nos falsitas verisimilis turbat. Non enim ea, sicut illa quae foris sunt, ullo sensu corporis tangimus, velut colores videndo, sonos audiendo, odores olfaciendo, sapores gustando, dura et mollia contrectando sentimus, quorum sensibilium etiam imagines eis simillimas, nec iam corporeas, cogitatione versamus, memoria tenemus, et per ipsas in istorum desideria concitamur: sed sine ulla phantasiarum vel phantasmatum imaginatione ludificatoria, mihi esse me, idque nosse et amare certissimum est.' (Aug. *De Civ. Dei*, xi. 26. Cf. *De Trin.* L. ix.)

'Habet anima in sua natura imaginem sanctae Trinitatis in eo quod intelligentiam, voluntatem et memoriam habet. Una est enim anima quae mens dicitur, una vita, et una substantia, quae haec tria habet in se: sed haec tria non sunt tres vitae; sed una vita; nec tres mentes sed una mens: consequenter utique nec tres substantiae sunt, sed una substantia . . . in his tribus

T

unitas quaedam est: intelligo me intelligere, velle, et meminisse; et volo me intelligere et meminisse et velle; et memini me intelligere et velle et meminisse.' (Alcuin, *De An. Rat.* 147.)

'Habet igitur mens rationalis cum se cogitando intelligit, secum imaginem suam ex se natam, id est cogitationem sui ad suam similitudinem, quasi sua impressione formatam, quamvis ipsa se a sua imagine non nisi ratione sola separare possit, quae imago eius verbum eius est. Hoc itaque modo, quis neget summam sapientiam, cum se dicendo intelligit, gignere consubstantialem sibi similitudinem suam, id est verbum suum? Quod verbum, licet de re tam singulariter eminenti proprie aliquid satis convenienter dici non possit, non tamen inconvenienter sicut similitudo, ita et imago, et figura et character eius dici potest.' (Anselm, *Monol.* c. xxxiii.)

THE END.

MACMILLAN & CO.'S WORKS ON THEOLOGY.

Memorials (Part I) Family and Personal, 1766-1865. By ROUNDELL, EARL OF SELBORNE. With Portraits and Illustrations. 2 vols. Demy 8vo, 25s. net.

SPEAKER.—'It has a very high historical value as well as a biographical interest—the latter interest including some graphic sketches of eminent contemporaries—and on certain historical points it promises to be an authority of the highest importance.'

Life and Letters of Fenton John Anthony Hort, D.D., D.C.L., LL.D., sometime Hulsean Professor and Lady Margaret's Reader in Divinity in the University of Cambridge. By his Son, ARTHUR FENTON HORT, late Fellow of Trinity College, Cambridge. In 2 vols. With Portrait. Extra Crown 8vo, 17s. net.

GUARDIAN.—'We have nothing but welcome for this memorial of Dr. Hort's life. . . . Mr. Hort has succeeded in giving to the world a vivid and striking picture of his distinguished father, and he is to be congratulated on the manner in which he has discharged his difficult duties as editor.'

Six Lectures on the Ante-Nicene Fathers. By the late Rev. F. J. A. HORT, D.D. Crown 8vo, 3s. 6d.

TIMES.—'Though certainly popular in form and treatment they are so in the best sense of the words, and they bear throughout the impress of the ripe scholarship, the rare critical acumen, and the lofty ethical temper which mark all Dr. Hort's work.'

Village Sermons Preached in the Parish Church of St. Ippolyts. By the late Rev. F. J. A. HORT, D.D. Crown 8vo. [*Shortly.*

The Early History of the Ecclesia. By the late Rev. F. J. A. HORT, D.D. Crown 8vo. [*Shortly.*

Documents Illustrative of English Church History. Compiled from Original Sources by HENRY GEE, B.D., F.S.A., and WILLIAM JOHN HARDY, F.S.A. Crown 8vo, 10s. 6d.

SCOTTISH GUARDIAN.—'There is no book in existence that contains so much original material likely to prove valuable to those who wish to investigate ritual or historical questions affecting the English Church.'

Outlines of Church History. By Prof. RUDOLF SOHM. Translated by Miss MAY SINCLAIR. With a Preface by Prof. H. M. GWATKIN, M.A. Crown 8vo, 3s. 6d.

EXPOSITOR.—'This little book has run through eight editions in six years in Germany, and we shall be surprised if it does not prove as acceptable and popular in its English dress. For we have nothing to compete with it. . . . It is a most delightful and instructive book.'

An Introduction to the Articles of the Church of England. By the Rev. G. F. MACLEAR, D.D., and Rev. W. W. WILLIAMS. Crown 8vo, 10s. 6d.

THE BISHOP OF PETERBOROUGH says:—'Seems to me to supply a decided want, and to contain much valuable information clearly put.'

THE BISHOP OF SALISBURY at the Church Congress spoke of this as 'a book which will doubtless have, as it deserves, a large circulation.'

Selections from Early Writers Illustrative of Church History to the Time of Constantine. By Prof. H. M. GWATKIN, M.A. Crown 8vo, 4s. net.

CHURCH QUARTERLY REVIEW.—'The students of our theological colleges ought to be grateful to Professor Gwatkin for bringing together in a handy form so many valuable passages.'

MACMILLAN AND CO., LTD., LONDON.

WORKS BY J. B. LIGHTFOOT, D.D.

Late Bishop of Durham.

Notes on Epistles of St. Paul from Unpublished Commentaries. 8vo. 12s.

St. Paul's Epistle to the Galatians. A Revised Text, with Introduction, Notes, and Dissertations. *Twentieth Thousand.* 8vo, 12s.

St. Paul's Epistle to the Philippians. A Revised Text, with Introduction, &c. *Nineteenth Thousand.* 8vo, 12s.

St. Paul's Epistles to the Colossians and to Philemon. A Revised Text, with Introductions, Notes, and Dissertations. *Fourteenth Thousand.* 8vo, 12s.

Dissertations on the Apostolic Age. Reprinted from the editions of St. Paul's Epistles. *Second Edition.* 8vo, 14s.

The Apostolic Fathers. PART I. **St. Clement of Rome.** A Revised Text, with Introductions, Notes, Dissertations, and Translations. *Second Edition.* 2 vols. 8vo, 32s.

The Apostolic Fathers. PART II. **St. Ignatius, St. Polycarp.** Revised Texts, with Introductions, Notes, Dissertations, and Translations. *Second Thousand.* 2 vols. in 3. 8vo, 48s.

The Apostolic Fathers. Abridged edition. With short Introductions, Greek Text, and English Translations. *Third Thousand.* 8vo, 16s.

Essays on the Work entitled 'Supernatural Religion.' *Second Edition.* 8vo, 10s. 6d.

On a Fresh Revision of the English New Testament. *Third Edition.* Crown 8vo, 7s. 6d.

Leaders in the Northern Church. Durham Sermons. *Fifth Thousand.* Crown 8vo, 6s.

Ordination Addresses and Counsels to Clergy. *Third Thousand.* Crown 8vo, 6s.

Cambridge Sermons. *Third Thousand.* Crown 8vo, 6s.

Sermons Preached in St. Paul's. *Third Thousand.* Crown 8vo, 6s.

Sermons on Special Occasions. *Second Thousand.* Crown 8vo, 6s.

Biblical Essays. *Second Thousand.* 8vo, 12s.

Historical Essays. Globe 8vo, 5s. [*Eversley Series.*

Index of Noteworthy Words and Phrases found in the Clementine Writings, commonly called the Homilies of Clement. 8vo, 5s.

Bishop Lightfoot. Reprinted from the *Quarterly Review.* With a Prefatory Note by the BISHOP OF DURHAM. With Portrait. Crown 8vo, 3s. 6d.

MACMILLAN AND CO., LTD., LONDON.

www.ingramcontent.com/pod-product-compliance
Lightning Source LLC
Chambersburg PA
CBHW032101230426
43672CB00009B/1603